# A JOURNEY WITH ME AS A:

# COWBOY
# WARRIOR
# LAWYER

## BY: BLUE GHOST 17

Memoir is always a search for self,

and everyone's personal story is rich in drama,

relationships, and surprising discoveries.

["Your life is a book by Brenda Peterson & Sarah Jane Freymann]


Ralph Waldo Emerson is often credited with the following:

*Life is a journey, not a destination.*

**To:**

**LINDA JEAN**

Please have your friends get a copy:

Go to:

blueghost17.com

Or

llrealtypublishing.com

Copyrighted 2016

**Paperback**
**ISBN-** 978-0-9981377-0-4
**Hardback**
**ISBN-**978-0-9981377-2-8
**E-Book**
**ISBN-**9780998137711

All rights reserved by L L Realty Publishing and Distribution Company.

Hughes YOH-6A Cayuse US Army in flight, public domain, used with permission.

"Leather cowboy boots and hat," Shutterstock.com ©ppart;

"Wood texture background," Shutterstock.com © Ksw Photographer;

"Wooden brown gavel," Shutterstock.com © Alex Staroseltsev;

Book cover design by Suzanne Parrott

Book Editor: Katharine Worthington and Tonya Blust

# TABLE OF CONTENTS

1. INTRODUCTION………………………..….7

## MENTORS

2. JEWELL'S COALDALE……………………......….……..13

3. CARL'S RO RANCH……………………….…………..23

4. BEKO'S TONOPAH………………….….………....29

## COWBOY TIMES

5. SADDLE UP……….…....…………………….33

6. BUCKAROO GROWING YEARS………..37

7. COWBOY STORIES…………..…………..43

8. THE ELEMENTS AND WATER…………..48

9. POOR SETTLERS………..…..…………….53

10. RANCH WORK……..…..……………….60

11. MOVING COWS……………..………….69

12. CLOVERDALE……………………….…..73

13. LAST MEMORIES OF RANCH LIFE…….78

## WARRIOR TIMES

14. START YOUR AIRCRAFT……………..….85

15. PREDESTINED……....………..…..………89

16. HELLO VIETNAM…………………..….…100

17. ACTS OF VALOR……………………..…115

18. COWBOY VS WARRIOR……..….…..…132

19. RETURN TO BASE…………...…….…,138

20. HIDDEN TRUTHS……..…………..…....144

## LAWYER TIMES

21. YOU MAY PROCEED COUNSELOR….150

22. LEAVING THE ARMY……………….....152

23. THE TRANSITION……………….…….159

24. PRACTICE OF LAW BEGINS………….166

25. STARTING A SOLO PRACTICE……...174

26. ART OF PERSUASION PART ONE…..186

27. ART OF PERSUASION PART TWO….214

28. LAW PRACTICE ENDS IN A
    WHIRLWIND……………………………..230

29. REFLECTING……………...……………240

# INTRODUCTION

The chronicles that follow detail memories of life as a young boy growing up in Coaldale Junction, a small, isolated community in central Nevada, with a lone truck stop, a bar, a restaurant, and a motel owned by Jewel and Elton Parsons. Jewell my maternal grandmother, and Elton, Jewell's second marriage, but the only grandfather I knew. Coaldale Junction sits at the intersection of Highways 6 and 95, 40 miles from Tonopah and 30 miles from Mina, the closest towns. It is right in the middle of the Nevada desert: sagebrush fields, alkaloid salt marshes, and no fresh drinking water.

These memoirs focus first on my childhood and adolescent efforts to become a cowboy on my uncle's cattle ranch, and then on my days as a combat helicopter pilot in Vietnam. In the final section, I recount the trials and tribulations I went through to become a successful lawyer in the "Cow Counties" (in other words, the counties of central Nevada) while struggling to deal with my war memories.

You will see how each of these stages of my life had an impact on the ones that followed, how these careers coalesced to form the person I became. The events and accounts are real, although I will note that memory fades and some of the details are missing. But the core is true.

I must confess

> The "true" cowboy has the right to claim that he has never been bucked off a horse; that he has never been outsmarted by a cow; and that he won his belt buckle at the rodeo.
>
> The "true" warrior is the best pilot who fears nothing, and who can fly anything that goes into the sky.
>
> The "true" lawyer will state that a trial was never lost through any fault of his. Another lawyer has never outsmarted him, and he knows pretty much everything.

My developmental days as a "wannabe" buckaroo will introduce you to the majestic valleys, mountain canyons and high meadows of Big Smoky Valley, in central Nevada — namely the RO Ranch, then owned by my uncle and mentor, Carl Haas.

The sights and scents of the towering mountains, open prairies, and spectacular sagebrush in bloom would take your breath away.

My attendance of high school at San Rafael Military Academy in San Rafael California giving me a chance to excel in the military structure, setting me up for what I thought would be a lifelong military career.

Later, I made it through the four-year Reserve Officers' Training Corps (ROTC) program at the University of Nevada. I received a commission as a second lieutenant in the United States Army Field Artillery Branch. After I had completed the officer basic course, I applied for flight school. Once I passed the flight physical, I was accepted into the Army aviation program. After completing the course, I was ordered to Vietnam.

Vietnam would be an experience that would only not be like anything I had faced, but a taxing tour of duty that changed my life forever. Yet, through skill and luck, I would survive, and my first orders were to return to Ft. Rucker and get into the instructor pilot course. After that, I would teach instrument flying for my last year of active duty. Becoming an instructor pilot came in handy, because after being admitted into law school, I was able to work as an instructor pilot with the National Guard during the day while attending law school at night at Sacramento's University of the Pacific McGeorge School of Law. After graduation from law school, I passed the Nevada state bar exam. A couple of years as Deputy District Attorney, and then had a private practice with public defender contracts for over 35 years.

In this book, I describe the situations that brought me laughter, tears, and fears as I moved through life. As you read, you will feel like you were there with me. My words will allow you to experience the sounds, the sights and the smells of each incident.

Some events of the war changed my life forever; at times these situations felt insurmountable. However, relying on the skills I had learned, as well as on my intuition and my ability to take the right action at the right time, I persevered and did not come home in a box. Read closely to understand how each stage allowed me to understand and face the consequences of my actions.

My stories sometimes include the trauma of death and having to kill or be killed. These scenes will allow you to understand how I had to learn to hate to survive.

Finally, I describe the real trials and tribulations, of becoming a lawyer in the Cow Counties. My goal was to serve my clients while becoming calmer and forgiving myself for my past actions and for being the person I had to become in combat.

I slowly stopped dwelling on the past and began looking forward to what good I could do for people. The sorrow over what I did and over the loss of comrades remains deeply embedded within, but it no longer causes deep depression or drives me to the bottle.

These sounds, smells, and visions are unforgettable. They are forever sealed within my heart and soul.

Of enduring memory, also, are the common threads running through all three walks of life. I needed to be accepted as a competent horseman and trusted cowboy; I desired to be an exceptional pilot, able to perform feats with an aircraft that no one knew could be done; and I strove to become an astute attorney, able to ask questions of a witness who was unaware she was being led hopelessly into a corner. I would get the answers I wanted. I would gain respect from opposing counsel, and from the judge.

Even more central, fundamental, and inherent in my struggle as a cowboy, a warrior, and a lawyer was – and has been – my dedication to learn specific skills coupled with instant, intuitive, correct actions. This focus provides the backbone for facing an ever-changing reality. But what lies behind this demanding need to excel? The answers will unfold as you read on!

I was surprised to discover that a common thread runs through each period of my life. That thread is my dependence on stamina, focus, and dedication, as well as an unexplainable instant, intuitive ability to take the right action at the right time. Oh, and there was just plain good luck... or, sometimes, bad luck!

My learned careful attentiveness around animals and machinery on the ranch proved invaluable in combat conditions. These skills even helped me deal with the tricks and occasional backstabbing tactics of opposing counsel in the courtroom.

I tender to you that, as a cowboy, a warrior, and a lawyer, I know that "life must be taken with a grain of salt." It is the living – not the destination – that makes a life. This idea is far more ingeniously expressed in the poems of the famous Rubaiyat of Omar Khayyam, the Astronomer-Poet of Persia, translated by Edward Fitzgerald:

> Oh, threats of Hell and Hopes of Paradise!
> One thing at least is certain—This life flies;
> One thing is certain, and the rest is Lies;
> The Flower that once has blown forever dies.

---

> The Moving Finger writes; and, having writ,
> Moves on: nor all thy Piety nor Wit
> Shall lure it back to cancel half a Line,
> Nor all thy Tears wash out a Word of it."

---

> Yesterday This Day's Madness did Prepare;
> To-morrow's Silence, Triumph, or Despair:
> Drink! For you know not whence you came, nor why;
> Drink! For you know not why you go, nor where.

We cannot go through life without being able to laugh and cry or to learn to face the consequences or to see how our calamities and triumphs are so similar. To pass on to you, my experiences as a modern-day cowboy raises my spirits and solidifies those stories forever. The variety of events, challenges, and beauties of "cowboying" may open your eyes to life's simple pleasures. How crystal-clear my memories became during the writing process!

We can't ignore the actions of war; we must examine them so that we can understand why such conduct and violence between humans happens. I find it difficult to disclose the deep emotions I developed in the combat environment. I am sure I am no different from any other young man or woman who has faced such struggles. Perhaps my stories will lead you to empathize with those young men or women who have PTSD. When you see a young man or woman in uniform, please thank them for their service.

My stories about the legal system and the struggles between adversaries testify to the importance of men and women living together in society and not harming each other. Yet, emotions and the art of persuasion are also critical to the outcome.

While reading this book, imagine yourself experiencing these events.

- Listening to the old cowboy's tales at the dinner table, or around the campfire.
- Feeling the fears and hopes of being in a war in which killing or being killed were the stakes at hand.
- Looking at a jury that must be convinced that the accused did not commit the crime for which he was charged, even if it means discrediting the crying fourteen-year-old witness.

SIT BACK, READ, AND ENJOY.

# MENTORS

# JEWELL'S COALDALE

As far back as my memory allows, I have held a deep love for my grandmother, Jewell, and her delightful desert truck stop, known as Coaldale. My parents divorced when I was a couple of months old, so my mother, sister and I moved in with her mother, Jewell.

Coaldale was a business in the middle of the Nevada desert consisting of a truck stop, a gas station, a restaurant, a bar, and, later, a motel. I grew up there and attended grade school in the nearby community of Tonopah. Such was my connection to this placed that while I attended San Rafael Military High School, I picked up the nickname "Coaldale Kid."

I vividly recall being awakened by the rumble of the diesel trucks parked next to the bar and café at Coaldale Junction. The truck stop was nestled on the edge of Columbus Marsh in central Nevada, about halfway between Las Vegas and Reno. The summer heat often exceeded 110 degrees. Then, at night the temperature would dip to 40 degrees. Sweating as I dug ditches or repaired the roof, I could see the snow on the White Mountains to the west. There were no trees to block the wind, so when it blew, all the sand and dirt went freewheeling. It was a common occurrence to clean the entire café and, in the next instant, find two inches of sand on the tables. The only available water was salty, okay for washing clothes (adding a little vinegar would cut the salt) and bathing. Our drinking water was brought down in a water trailer from Dicalite Minerals Corporation, 14 miles up the road to the west at Montgomery Pass. Everyone living at Coaldale remembered to fill little containers for their night's drinking water.

Coaldale was so named because there was a coal mine about three miles away, within the southern hills. The quality of the coal was so bad that the mine didn't last long.

The original owner/developer, Carl Rieke, had great plans for Coaldale; he had a plat map of Coaldale recorded at the county office, but the town never developed. It started out as Carl's Place in the twenties and was a water stop for the rail line running from Virginia City to the mining towns of Tonopah and Goldfield. The train service was discontinued in the early forties, and the tracks were removed. The railhead was in Mina, about 30 miles north; that was not abandoned until the late seventies. The major user of the railhead was Dicalite Minerals Corporation, transporting diatomous earth to customers.

In the early years, very few cars traveled the road, so you were aware of the stillness in the desert, unlike anywhere else. You could hear only the sound of a cricket or two at the end of the sewer drain pipe, or a lone coyote or jackrabbit running across the road. When the sage was in bloom, marvelous natural perfume permeated the air. The big, open sky at night made the observer feel like a pebble of sand in the grand scheme of things. No street lights, and, in the early days, if the generator went out, there were no lights at all. Out came the kerosene lamps and candles.

I spent my early school days at Coaldale. A nine-passenger station wagon driven by a teacher who lived in Fish Lake Valley would take us the 40 miles to the school in Tonopah. When not in school or at my uncle's ranch, I learned to pump gas, make beds, and fix almost anything. Later, during breaks from college, I became a bartender, a trade that would later bring in extra cash for me in Reno. I recall breaking up many a fight amongst the construction workers who stayed in the motels at Coaldale. When not working, there was not much to do in Coaldale except drink and fight.

As the "Coaldale Kid," I never needed my grandmother to wake me up in the early morning. No matter how quietly she tried to open the back door to the main building, I would hear the squeak. I would then jump out of bed and quickly get dressed so I could help her sweep and clean. My job was to scatter sawdust over the hardwood floor while Jewell swept. The sawdust would pick up any wet or greasy spills on the floor. I wanted to help, even as young as six years old, because I knew my grandmother had worked late cooking and tending bar for the truckers and tourists traveling to and from Las Vegas and Reno.

Like so many young boys from broken homes and with no father figure, I turned to the one guiding light, a non-judgmental and enduring source of support and encouragement, a disciplinarian, and a comforter in sad times: my grandmother!

I so admired this delightful lady. She worked very hard and taught me to do the same. She was a great shot with a pistol or rifle, and always had a gun in the side drawer of her nightstand. She never smoked, so, because she was my role model, I never smoked either.

Her principal disciplinary instrument was a single willow switch to "tan the backside." I would get a spanking when I was caught climbing the water tower or the windmill. I got a good one when I tried to start a bonfire under my bed. When I was seven, my grandmother caught me taking her pistol from the bedstand and firing it at a lizard a couple of times. She had taught me early on how to use a gun, but I was not to take it out by myself. It took only a couple of swats with the switch, and the message was clear that this conduct would not be tolerated. Aside from the fact that these spankings helped shape my future conduct and taught me to respect authority, I now realize that it showed me that you must face the consequences of your actions. I quickly learned right from wrong. In my heart, I knew these spankings were dispensed with Jewell's unconditional love, one that would last a lifetime, and that is still preserved deep within my inmost memories.

Oh, those memories of working with her in the washroom, still using a scrub board and cranking the rollers to squeeze the water out of the garment. I remember that if I put too much clothing in at a time, the roller would come apart, requiring Jewell to take out her hand "fix-anything kit" and re-connect the rollers.

When it came time to hang the clothes on the clothesline to dry, I was too short to do it, so Jewell would grab an empty apple crate for me to stand on. The refreshing smell of the freshly cleaned clothes and sheets remains in my mind today.

What joy flashed in her eyes when the first electric washing machine and dryer arrived! The new machinery, however, brought a bit of emptiness because when the contraptions replaced the washtubs and scrub board, I lost those times of laughter, of hearing my grandma's amazing stories, and the many hours of washing clothes until our hands were as wrinkled as prunes. No more rhythmic sounds of her scraping the material on the scrub board as though she were improvising a song.

I also have memories of helping her clean the guest rooms in the motel. I remember, as clearly today, those days when I would help make the beds. I can visualize my grandmother on the other side of the bed, correcting me if the sheets were not perfect or if the bottom was not tucked in exactly right. I remember this so vividly that I often have the inclination to reach out and touch her hand when I am making my bed today.

The bed-making lessons proved invaluable at military school. The other newbies had to be taught to make their beds correctly. This mandatory requirement, however, was a piece of cake for the Coaldale Kid.

That was just one of many lessons imparted by my grandmother that would dramatically affect my life. Her demand for perfection led me to seek the same in the military and my law practice. Her ability to stay on course and reach goals also set me up for success in the fields I pursued. The only thing I lacked was her kindness!

When I was young, I would pull the apple crate next to the stove so that I was tall enough to stir the gravy, intent on making sure there were no lumps. I went on to cook for the cowboys at the ranch, then for the flight crew while at summer camp with the National Guard. I learned simple tricks, such as knowing that you could heat a jelly roll on a grill by laying it on a piece of lettuce and covering it with a lid. I soon learned to cook a breakfast of eggs, ham, bacon, sausage, and steak for a large group. I also learned to bake cakes, biscuits, and cookies. By age 14, I could cook a full dinner, including salads, soups, and meat.

Even today, when cooking is a therapeutic and relaxing hobby, I often feel as though Jewell is standing next to me, making sure the stove is not turned up too high, or that the oven is turned off after use. When cleaning the frying pans, I still make sure they are perfect, as if expecting a scolding from my grandma.

Learning to cook paid off especially well when I was thrown from a horse while I worked at the ranch. I injured my back and could hardly walk; there was no way I could ride for a while. Surprisingly, the day of my accident, the camp cook got drunk and quit. Therefore, I became the ranch cook while I rehabilitated. That meant cooking three meals a day for 10 to 12 ranch hands and cowboys. Up at 4:30 every morning, I learned new ways to cook. There is one lesson every camp cook should learn: When using an old gas stove, always, always find the matches first; then light the burner! It took only a few instances of scorching my eyebrows and the hair on my arms for me to remember that process. But I could always depend on the golden rule that everyone on a ranch knows: You never, ever complain about the food or the cook. The cook's revenge could be fatal.

Jewell, orphaned at eight years old, was not allowed to complete high school. She had to work long hours at a boarding house for a woman who took her in from the orphanage, not out of love, but for her labor. Attending school was not a chore for Jewell; she loved to learn. It wasn't all positive, though; my grandmother had to tolerate the primitive methods of the teachers, who would slap her left hand with a ruler when she attempted to write with it. Using your left hand for writing was not accepted in those days. After leaving the school, she used her left hand to write and developed the prettiest penmanship I have ever seen.

After the hard times in the boarding house days, Jewell fell in love with a rough-and-tough heavy equipment operator named Carl Haas. Though I never met my natural grandfather until late in high school when he visited the ranch for a couple of weeks, I was told that Carl Sr. was a mountain of a man. However, he turned out to not be the family man Jewell needed to help her overcome her earlier hardships. His bad behavior only added to the adversities she had encountered over the years. He worked hard, drank whiskey hard, and fought hard. Carl had a bad habit of finding a job some distance away, even in another state. He would up and leave Jewell and their two children, my uncle and my mother, to fend for themselves.

Jewell recalled taking on a job riding fences for income. Carl Jr., not more than three or four, was loaded on the back of the horse and told to hold on tight, and off they went in the hot summer or freezing winter. Little Carl declared, "Mommy, Mommy, you can run, you can walk, but please, please don't trot."

When Carl Jr. (her son) and Yvonne (her daughter and my mother) were very young, Jewel often had to rope a half-wild cow and tie it to the fence so she could squeeze half a tomato can of milk out of it. The one-room shack where she and the kids lived had no insulation, nor any interior water or toilet facilities. By herself, Jewel repaired the outhouse, fixed and insulated the hand-operated water pump, and even nailed cardboard to the sides of the walls to keep the wind from coming through the cracks – all while she tried to find work to feed her kids. That was because Carl, when away on a job, would usually gamble with the money and not send her any.

Another hard job she took on, for a dollar a day, was digging out trees that were then cut in half to make water troughs by hand. She would bend over, swinging a hoe and digging out the tough tree, chip by chip.

Jewell was finally able to get a job and a decent house at Carl's Place in Coaldale. Carl once again left them to take a job out of town. She would cook, tend bar, clean, and do pretty much anything Old Carl Reake wanted her to do.

The business consisted of one long room with a bar. There were swinging doors separating the bar from the kitchen area. A large table for family-style meals filled most of the kitchen area. Out front was an old hand gas pump with a glass cylinder. You would put the gas up and fill the cylinder with the desired amount (one gallon, two gallons, up to five gallons), then stick the handle at the end of a hose into the tank and fill up the car.

Jewell did most of that work after 5:00 p.m. so she could drive a truck for Dicalite Minerals Corporation, 14 miles west of Coaldale, at its open-pit mining operation. Workers would load the sacks of diatomaceous earth (a white, powdery substance used as a filtration aid, a metal polish, and even toothpaste) at the mine. Jewell would drive from there to Mina, about 50 miles south. The sacks were then unloaded and placed in railroad cars at the last remaining railhead.

It didn't take Jewell long to divorce Carl once the children were in high school and she felt that they could deal with it. It did not cause much trouble because Carl was seldom around anyway.

My grandmother told me a couple of funny stories about my grandfather. On one occasion, after a week-long drinking jag, Carl came crawling back, asking for forgiveness. This event occurred somewhere in New Mexico, long before she arrived at Coaldale. My grandmother forgave him, but it wasn't long before he decided to move again for another job. They loaded what few items they had into his old pickup truck, and off they went. The moon was extraordinarily bright that night when they had a flat tire. Jewell suggested that Carl check the "stim" on the tire because often a little pebble got caught in there and the tire would lose air. Carl would not let a woman tell him what was wrong, so he started jacking up the rig and pulling off the tire.

Suddenly, Carl cried for Jewell's help. He was sitting on the ground, still as a rock, whining: "Jewell, look! My arm is turning black, what is happening?" Jewell could hardly keep from laughing. She explained, "It is evident that all the times you left us, the drunkenness, the fighting, and the gambling away what money we had caused this. It is your lifestyle that has caused this darkness in your skin." Carl cried, "Oh, I promise I will change; I will do better!" Soon the blackness went away.

Carl never realized that the bright moonlight had created a shadow on his arm. To make matters even more comical, after breaking the tire completely down and finding no leaks, Carl checked the "stim." Sure enough, a pebble had gotten stuck in it, causing the air to get out. Carl got so mad, he took out his knife and stabbed the tire. Then he had to patch it and pump it up.

Carl Jr. related another incident about his father. Apparently, after being out of work for a while, Carl Sr. got a job operating a Caterpillar D8 tractor. He took pride in being one of the best in the business at working with this particular piece of machinery. On the first day, Carl and his son went to the job site, where they met the foreman. After the superintendent had explained to Carl what needed to be done for the day, Carl got on the Cat, started it, made Carl Jr. sit beside him, and started moving earth.

Carl then noticed that the foreman had come back to the job site in his pickup truck, watching how his new employee was doing. Carl told his son, "What in the Hell is he doing coming around here checking on me? I know what the job is, I have been doing this for years. I don't need him coming around and gawking at me." Soon the foreman left and Carl continued pushing earth with the bulldozer. Later, however, he again looked up and saw that the foreman had returned to check on the job. Carl worked himself into a mad frenzy, declaring, "I do not have to put up with this constant harassment! I am tired of that SOB coming around." He threw the gearshift into neutral, leaped off the Cat, ran over, and jumped on the sideboard of the foreman's pickup. He grabbed the foreman with one hand and hit him with the other. The foreman gunned the gas pedal and across the desert went the pickup truck, Carl still hanging onto the side and punching the foreman. Finally, after a couple of high bumps, Carl was thrown off. He picked himself off the sand, dusted himself off, and walked over to the Cat. He took Carl

Jr.'s hand and walked to his truck. My uncle softly added, "That job didn't last long."

Such was the temperament of Carl Sr., and one of the reasons why Jewell got a divorce. Yet the divorce did not slow her down. How could it? She had managed to survive on her own with the kids for years. So, she and her children settled down. My mother and uncle completed high school in Tonopah. Jewell continued working two jobs, driving the truck during the day and working in the bar and kitchen at night.

After some time, Carl Reake gave Jewell the option to buy the business. She had saved up enough money for a down payment, and could pay off the balance in a short time. Sadly, however, shortly after she did this, old Carl Reake walked drunkenly across the road to his house and was run over by a car. The driver could not see the old man in the dark of night. Carl, being drunk, probably never saw the car coming, even though one could see more than five miles each way down the open stretch of road on a clear night or day. Carl Reake died and Jewell owned Coaldale.

Jewell continued to do well at Coaldale, later moving the establishment closer to the junction. That way, traffic going from Tonopah to Bishop would not have to drive the one mile from the turn-off.

Jewell would later marry Elton Parson, whom she loved for nearly 30 years before her death. Together they would not falter in their mutual love for Coaldale, even in 1970, when a fire started in their trailer, next to the bar and café. The fire spread; within minutes all was a giant ball of flame. Her home, the trailer, the bar, the gas station, and the café were gone: a pile of burnt rubble. The heat was so intense that Jewell could not even grab her purse from around the corner of the entrance to her trailer. Everything they owned was destroyed except for the clothes on their backs.

Fortunately, the small amount of insurance was enough to purchase the old hospital building in Tonopah. They paid to have it moved to Coaldale. Elton's construction company did most of the work to rebuild the foundation and electrical system, and the buildings were joined to make the new Coaldale. Within four months, Coaldale was back in full swing. This time, Jewell and Elton had a great two-bedroom apartment built in the main building.

Jewel was always involved in politics. She was appointed to the prestigious Fish and Gaming Commission. She was elected to a couple of terms as commissioner of Esmeralda County and ultimately elected state legislator for Mineral, Nye, and Esmeralda counties.

Jewell died in 1983, but not before having an indelible, permanent impact and influence on me as a young cowboy, warrior, and lawyer. Her "never-give-up" attitude stuck with me. She taught me that all a person needs is the willingness to set his or her goals and pursue them with firm conviction and unfettered determination. Do not let bends in the road deter you. People can be cruel and often inhibit your path with jealousy. Ignore these distractions, stay the course, and you will succeed.

These lessons would frequently ring true when, as a young cowboy, I faced challenges on the cattle ranch. Jewell's words would resonate when, as a young warrior, I had to go on a combat mission. It was difficult to avoid the persistent thought, 'I may die today,' but her words made me stay the course and "cowboy up."

So often at law school and in my law practice, I would remember Jewell's words. Each day while working, and also while writing this book, I constantly think of Jewell — the love she had for me, the example she set, and the lessons she taught. Even after 30 years, I can clearly remember her warm smile; the hint of her perfume; her many dresses, all with colorful floral designs; the warm touch of her hand; the obvious love in her eyes.

 **Jewell in the early years.**

# CARL'S RO RANCH

I still have crystal-clear memories of my early days at the ranch. I recall my Uncle Carl shouting down the hall, "Rise and shine! Are you going to sleep the day away?" Of course, this was 4:00 a.m., when the day began on the working ranch. Carl gave me no slack as a young buckaroo, a "wannabe cowboy." I am infinitely grateful to have had an uncle so instrumental in shaping my destiny as a cowboy, a warrior, and a lawyer. How could I have ever predicted that the guidance he gave me at such a young age would prove invaluable on the battlefield and in the courtroom?

The RO Ranch was 60 miles from Coaldale, so my grandmother could take me there often to visit my uncle and pursue my dream of becoming a cowboy.

Carl had the foresight to purchase the RO Ranch, a cattle ranch with over a million acres of grazing rights. On the home spread, the RO could hold 3500 head of livestock in the pens, running 1800 mother cows. There were 6900 deeded acres, 2100 of which were irrigated pasture.

Carl later purchased smaller spreads at Cloverdale, Pevine, Wineglass, and Barney Mainer ranches. These were little working ranches, most likely created under the Homestead Act in the late 1860s. They were similar: a small two-bedroom ranch house, a corral, a barn, an outhouse, and usually a windmill.

Carl operated his ranches the old-fashioned way — by moving cows with a horse. No fancy cattle trucks or horse trailers. Just horses, pack mules, an old chuck wagon, and lariats. I needed to work hard and take care of my horse to gain the respect of the other cowhands.

In my early days of being a wannabe buckaroo, I spent a couple of weeks each summer, some Christmas vacations, and Easter at the RO, starting at six years of age. After age 12, I spent all my summer and winter holidays at the ranch. By that time, I could handle almost any task assigned, even though I was often called a "sawed-off runt." I had spent many years learning specific chores: feeding the chickens, horses, and pigs; milking cows; digging up potatoes; slaughtering steer; or killing a chicken for dinner. I would pick the tomatoes, corn, apples, and any other fruit produced by the little orchard. The memory of the sweet smells and tastes of the garden-fresh produce and fruit are still ingrained in my brain.

Carl was willing to take a chance on me — to let this "runt" of a kid grow and expand by doing, not watching; such as driving tractor. Once, when I was backing the tractor to hook up a hay wagon, Carl held the tongue of the wagon so I could attach it to the tractor. My short legs would not reach the clutch to stop the backward movement while I was turned around. Thus, I smashed Carl's leg between the tractor and the hay wagon. The injury was not bad, but it served as a hard lesson: I had to learn how to stay straight to reach the clutch when backing up.

There were many other memorable experiences, like when I ran my horse a little too fast; when it turned off, I flew headfirst into the dirt. Or the time when I walked a little too close to that nervous horse and got kicked in the side. Most of these events occurred only once.

One of the worst things I did was lose my work gloves.

The reason that was so bad was that when handling machinery, hay hooks, or roping, if one didn't wear good, sturdy gloves, one was prone to splinters, bruises, cuts, and dirt. Just another lesson quickly learned and not easily forgotten. Even to this day, knowing where I left my work gloves is a necessity of life.

Carl also provided a most inspiring way to improve my self-confidence. Carl would not let me give up or get mad and quit when I performed a task poorly. "Do it right or keep doing it until you get it right" was Carl's mantra.

When I began attending school, I had no real confidence in my learning abilities; I had difficulty learning to read and spell. I even had to repeat the third grade. But on one winter vacation, Carl decided to work with me on memory, reading, and spelling. Carl decided we would dissect every word of Edgar Allan Poe's "The Raven." We looked up each word, examining why the author picked that word or phrase and asking what other words could be used instead. It was inspiring and compelling. This process affected me like a bolt of lightning. I began understanding and analyzing words, and learned to read and spell properly. Suddenly, I knew I had the ability to learn and do well in school. I just needed confidence. I graduated from high school on the honor roll. To this day, as an old lawyer, I can still recite passages from Poe's classic poem. Most importantly, those lessons gave me the necessary self-assurance to realize that I could tackle any kind of school work as well as ranch work, be it military high school, the University of Nevada, the Officers' Training Corps, Army aviation school, flight instructor training, and, of course, McGeorge School of Law.

How lucky I was to have such support and to take advantage of it. So many times, as a public defender, I interviewed troubled youths, knowing that if they had had any kind of support system, they would not have been involved in criminal activities. So often they would plead for help, but their parents or family members were not there, mainly because they were too stoned on drugs to know or care.

I remember to this day a poem Carl taught me ("Another Way" by Ambrose Bierce):

> I lay in silence, dead. A woman came
>    And laid a rose upon my breast, and said,
> "May God be merciful." She spoke my name,
>    And added, "It is strange to think him dead.
>
> "He loved me well enough, but 'twas his way
>    To speak it lightly." Then, beneath her breath:
> "Besides"—I knew what further she would say,
>    But then a footfall broke my dream of death.
>
> Today the words are mine. I lay the rose
>    Upon her breast, and speak her name, and deem
> It strange indeed that she is dead. God knows
>    I had more pleasure in the other dream.

It wasn't until age 12 that I was given the opportunity to work with the other cowboys in round-ups, herding cattle from the desert plains in winter to the high mountain meadows in spring. Though I was still short, I became strong and tough as nails. I could "buck" 50-pound hay bales with my arms and knees, using the force of the bales as I pulled them off the loader. It was a feat to be able to stack them six rolls high. I learned to drive the hay trucks, the tractors, the bailer, and even an old Massey-Harris combine.

By age 14, there was no assignment I couldn't do, and do well. I was gaining the respect of my uncle as well as of the other cowboys.

There were very hard times moving cows in 100-degree summer temperatures or in the cold sub-zero weather of winter, especially in a blinding snow storm. But I "cowboyed-up" and persevered.

The ability to handle many fearful occurrences on the ranch made the dangers of war more manageable. Indeed, it seemed that war's terrors did not affect me as much as they did the other pilots or gunner/crew chiefs who didn't have ranch work experience.

Though my connection with Carl was close, there was an element of sadness in our relationship after my grandmother's death. My stepgrandfather, Elton Parsons, was to inherit Coaldale, the business Jewell had spent her life building. My mother and Uncle Carl thought they should have that asset. I was caught in the middle. Elton was the only grandfather I knew. I knew of Elton and Jewell's loving relationship, and how they both had fought to keep Coaldale alive, especially after the fire in 1970. The legal battle included a bitter contest that went to the Nevada Supreme Court. Such situations never have a winner; they only break up a family for life. Elton retained Coaldale, and my relationship with Carl ended because of my stance.

The RO was a warm and caring place that lives on in my heart and soul. The hours spent in the saddle, though difficult, constitute some of the fondest memories of my life.

Luckily my rift with Carl did not occur until I was firmly settled in my law practice in central Nevada. Carl could witness how I went from the serenity of ranch life to the discipline of the college preparatory school at San Rafael Military Academy, then my studies at the University of Nevada, and the ROTC program where I became an Army officer. Carl supported all my endeavors. He even paid for a beautiful weekend in San Francisco for my wife and me a week before I shipped out to Vietnam.

My gratitude for what Carl gave me has never waned, and I feel shame and regret over the foolishness of our fighting. Not long before his death, however, we were able to meet for a quiet lunch. We laughed, cried, and just sat quietly, reminiscing about the many ranch adventures we had experienced together. That was the last time I saw Carl, and I am glad, because that's the way I want to remember him. Even today, long after Carl's death, I will never forget that his support and actions not only shaped me but most likely saved my life when I faced combat decisions.

# BEKO'S TONOPAH

The former great mining town in central Nevada, known as Tonopah.

I attended grade school in Tonopah. As I mentioned previously, one of the school's teachers, who lived in Fish Lake Valley, used a nine-passenger car, purchased by my grandmother, to pick up kids who also lived in that valley (20 miles southwest of Coaldale), then take the kids living at Coaldale, 40 miles away. She would drive us to school and back. The long commute allowed us extra time to do our homework, sleep, or just visit. We would often listen to the only radio station available, transmitted out of Fallon.

As an elementary school student, I never imagined that this town of Tonopah would come to mean so much to me. As the pages of my life turned, it became clear that Tonopah was the starting point — not just the place where I graduated from eighth grade, but the launching pad for my legal career.

It was all because of a remarkable man named William P. Beko. Bill was the district attorney in Tonopah in the early fifties and sixties, and a great friend of Jewell's. When my grandmother and I went to Tonopah to shop or run errands, Jewell would drive to the old historic courthouse to see Bill Beko. I got to know him over the years. You must remember, Jewell was a politician and Beko was also one of the best.

Still, I did not recognize until 15 or 20 years later the dramatic impact Beko had on my life and my future. This impact would extend beyond his lifetime. Thanks to the strict guidance I received as his law clerk, and as a deputy district attorney when he was our district judge, my legal career thrived.

Tonopah is still remarkable to me. When I was young, I found it exciting because there were still visible signs of it being a grand old mining town: the old wooden derricks, the high stockpiles of processed earth, and the beautiful Mizpah Hotel. That hotel was refurbished in 1980 to its original condition from the 1800s.

During my ranch days, I would go into town with some of the other cowboys for occasions such as the Elks' annual dance, the firehouse fundraising dance, and, of course, the Fourth of July. Ken Siri, the game warden, would wrap half a steer in burlap sacks and cook it in the ground with hot rocks. The meat would melt in your mouth. The main street became a large party area with tables for people to eat, a country band, and a large dance floor. The festivities would go into the late evening hours. Bill always seemed to be the man in charge; he knew everyone by name. On one occasion, Bill called out every attendee's name, personally thanking them for contributing to the cause occasioned by the event.

Bill later became the district court judge. His circuit was the 5th Judicial District, with courthouses in Tonopah, Goldfield, and Hawthorne. He would often stop by Coaldale Junction to see Jewell, have a bite to eat, or fill up the car before going home to Tonopah after a late-night court trial or hearing. One of these stops would prove to be the most rewarding incident of my life.

Years later, while dealing with the Honorable William P. Beko I was constantly reminded of how much he had helped me and changed my life.

Judge Beko, to this day, holds a special place deep in my heart. Not only did Beko create a path for me to transition from a warrior to a lawyer, but he provided me with the solid footing to be a great.

It is difficult to find words that adequately express the gratitude I feel toward Judge Beko for how he changed my life and the lives of my family members.

Bill's passing was not only a huge loss for me, but for every member of the community. As far back as memory allows, I do not remember a larger crowd than the one that attended Bill's funeral, or my grandmother's.

# COWBOY TIMES

# SADDLE UP

Many challenges evolved into learning experiences during the summers and school vacations I spent at the RO Ranch in Smoky Valley, central Nevada. It had taken a while before I felt at ease when the cow boss gave the directive: "Saddle up."

The label of "cowboy" might make you think of lanky men in big hats and boots, battling wild Indians and swinging women around at square dances. The reality was more mundane – a cowboy spent a considerable amount of time moving cows from one place to another.

I distinctly recall the typical start of a workday. The primary job was to ride out find the cows herd, or drive them to another location, repeatedly. That is from the flat land to the mountain meadows or vice versa. There were also other tasks for the cowboys, most cowboys didn't like. They also had to fix fences, cleaning corrals or barns, and maintaining their "tack."

Then there were the horses! The day would break with the painstaking struggle of putting feed bags of grain over their heads so they could eat.

As the "kid" on the ranch, I found it was my job to grain the horses, all ten to fifteen of them. They would step on me, kick me, bite me, and shove me around as they fought to get their grain sack first.

As if that ordeal was not enough, I then had to lasso my mount for the day. Once caught, no matter how many times I did it, the horse would fight me when I tried to tack him up (i.e., put the bit in his mouth, the bridle on his face, and the saddle on his back). It took me a while to learn the tricks to outsmarting the horse. I would put one of the reins over the back of his head so that when the horse tried to pull his head away from the bit, I could shove it into his mouth; all I had to do was pull down firmly on the rein and the bit would quickly slid in.

Another trick was to back the horse against the fence when he tried to pull aside as I aimed the saddle and saddle blanket at his back. When he backed up and hit the wall, the saddle, pad, and blanket could be quickly placed on his back. I would firmly tighten the cinch to make sure the saddle stayed fast as I mounted him. That was a hard lesson learned. Due to a loose saddle, I found myself slammed to the ground a few times; I had put my foot in the stirrup — and around rolled the saddle.

I learned to walk my horse around a few times, making sure nothing was aggravating or pinching him before mounting. I also had to endure his bucking a few times when I would mistakenly place the scratchy saddle blanket before the pad. When I sat in the saddle, the weight would make the blanket scratch his back, and the bucking would begin. After learning all those lessons, I was ready to be a cowboy.

Then came the command from the cow-boss: "Saddle up!" In an instant, I reached up to grab a handful of mane. My right hand grasped the saddle horn, and I pulled myself up into the saddle. I stuck my left boot firmly into the stirrup, but not too far. I had learned over the years that my boot could be trapped in the stirrup, and I'd be dragged in the dust. Then, with a good, solid grip, I pulled myself completely into the saddle; my spurs sang out with a high-pitched tune as my right leg swung over the saddle, my right foot finding its way to the other stirrup. My long leather chaps made a crispy snapping sound as my leg hit the horse's flank. The horse's snort, the snap of the chaps and the tingling of the spurs abruptly interrupted the morning silence.

As I settled firmly into the saddle, weight evenly distributed on each stirrup, the horse lowered his head and arched his back as though he wanted to throw me off. After having ridden this horse for a long time, I knew his temperament, especially in the chilly early morning. I quickly pulled one rein tightly to the left so that the horse went in a circle a couple of times and then straightened out. The left turn ensured that I stayed on. Turning right would push me away from the horse, and it would be easy for him to throw me off.

I then gently nudged the horse with the spurs. Now the horse sensed who was in charge. I gave the horse a kick with the spurs or a slap on the rump with the reins, and off we went.

It was always quite a sight to see all the cowboys riding slowly out of the corral to round up the herd. The cowboys rode shoulder to shoulder, side by side — not in a line like you see in the movies. Each cowboy wore his own unique hat, spurs, and boots. Some rolled their own cigarettes. Some talked about their horses; others didn't say much at all, they would just enjoy the morning.

That was always the moment when I noticed the horizon sparkling with a bright golden color as the sun peeked over the mountains. Sometimes the clouds looked like dancing animals of all kinds. Elephants, giraffes, lions, bears – you name it. With the different lights and shadows, my imagination seemed to soar.  The dew on the sagebrush glistened like silver crystal.

I'd deeply inhale the morning air, anticipating the brilliant scent of desert sagebrush in full bloom. The spicy fragrance overwhelmed the senses.

As the sunlight brightened the sky, the stunning red, orange, and lavender of the blooming sage stretched over the prairie as far as the eye could see. These sights and smells made the 10-to-12-hour day in the saddle a little easier.

It would be a full day of chasing cows, dodging sagebrush and sand hills and evading the occasional rattlesnake, scorpion, lizard, or horny toad. At day's end, I pulled the saddle and blanket off the horse. I walked him around slowly to cool him. I then wet a towel and rubbed the sweat off his back. Some of the cowhands didn't take such good care of their animals. They would be tired and just remove the gear and put the horses back in the corral. Such a practice is what's meant by the old cowboy saying: "She looks like she'd been 'rode hard' and put away wet too many times." (That phrase was also sometimes used to describe the gals who hung out in the local bars.)

It would take me many years and many a hard knock before I could efficiently settle in and take complete control of the horse, to feel confident in moving a small herd of cows alone, and to accomplish the many chores of ranch work.

The ordeal complete, on this day and many days to come, the horse and cowboy would be ready to go, awaiting the encounters. But how many of these days would I face before I was accepted and became comfortable as a horseman, cattleman, and ranch worker?

These sights, sounds, and smells of the early morning "saddle-up" are eternally embedded in my heart and soul. Little did I know then that recalling these sights, sounds, and smells would help relieve my fears and nervousness when I faced tense combat situations.

# BUCKAROO GROWING YEARS

I can't forget the cold, wet winters on the ranch. I'm talking three-layers-of-Levi's-and-cotton-shirts, topped-with-a-poncho-raincoat cold — especially on top of a horse. Nor can I forget the summers, which were so dry and hot that one could fry an egg on the hood of the old '54 Chevy pickup truck we traveled in from water hole to water hole. My lips often became so dry and swollen that they cracked and bled. I specifically recall the time I lost my canteen. When I finally made it to the nearest well, I had to scatter the cows from the trough to fill my cup. As usual, the old windmill was not working and the old gas pump, made in the forties, wouldn't start.

Later in life, I was examined by an East Indian doctor, who asked if I had grown up on a farm. I told him yes, then asked him how he knew. He said, "Because you had a tapeworm when you were young! Most likely from drinking out of a trough." I told him about my chasing the cows away and getting water from the trough. He said, "Yes, that would do it."

I was five years old when the seasoned cowboy and cow boss -Ed Fisher helped me climb aboard my first horse. There was only one way to describe Ed — a horseman and cattleman, plain and straightforward. Ed explained, "The stirrups are used to steady yourself in the saddle, but put the toe of your boot only partially in – not all the way to the heel. If the boot is in all the way to the heel and you fall off, or get bucked or pulled off, there is a more likely chance that your foot will get stuck in the stirrup and the horse will drag you."

Ed's strictest rule was that my primary focus is caring for my horse. Don't jerk or pull hard on the reins — the bit is in the horse's mouth, which is tender; jerking or pulling hard will cause a sore. Hold the reins gently in your left hand; pull steadily backward, reins even, not hard, to stop the horse. Release them gently. Nudge the horse by striking your spurs into his side with the heel of your boots, and the horse will start moving forward. Hold your left hand centered over the saddle horn. You can increase his gait from a walk to a trot to a gallop, keeping the reins loose and nudging the horse with the heel of your boots or spurs. Gently move your hand to the left, causing the rein to put pressure on the right side of the horse's neck, and the horse will turn to the left. Move your hand to the right; the controlled pressure on the left side of the horse's neck will cause the horse to turn to the right.

This memory of the first day I ever sat on a horse is as vivid as if it had happened yesterday. How scared I was! The horse was so tall, with his big eyes, his tail swatting back and forth, his sharp frightening hooves, and his big teeth. I was a mile above the ground. I was sitting on a horse like the one in the song "Strawberry Roan" (a classic American cowboy song, written by California cowboy Curly Fletcher [1892-1954, and first published in 1915])

> "Down in the horse corral standin' alone
> Is an old Caballo, a Strawberry Roan
> His legs are all spavined, he's got pigeon toes
> Little pig eyes and a big Roman nose
> Little pin ears that touched at the tip
> A big 44 brand was on his left hip
> U-necked and all, with a long, lower jaw
> I could see with one eye, he's a regular outlaw."

Reassuringly, Ed Fisher, calmed me down as he lengthened the stirrups. He led the horse gently around the corral. I soon learned that the horse was very gentle. A simple tug on the reins and the gigantic horse would instantly stop. Ed continued to remind me: Hold the reins in the left hand. Move slightly to the left; the horse will turn to the left. Slightly to the right, the horse will turn right. Gently loosen the reins and the horse will move forward

It would take several years of falls and scary events before I felt totally comfortable on horseback. I learned about caring for my horse and equipment: saddle, bridle, lariat, and working gloves were all part of the business of becoming a cowboy. When I reached seven or eight years of age, Ed made me my first saddle and gave me my own set of spurs. He showed me how to care for them. I would oil the leather of the saddle occasionally and always place it gently on the wooden mount in the barn. I hung the bridle on the wall and properly coiled my lariat.

As each summer passed, I was assigned more and more tasks. Feeding the chickens, and pigs, milking cows, and everything else became second nature. I was around 14 when I was finally given primary duties. I could now fill the feed bags and place them on the heads of all the work horses. I could saddle my own horse. Set the pad first, then place the saddle blanket squarely on the saddle. Pull the cinch tightly under the horse and securely latch it to the side with a flat knot. My spurs were fastened to my boots with a beautiful leather strap, and a piece of baling wire was tied to each side and slipped under the heel. My chaps were the length of my legs, modified by Ed to suit my size. Slowly, I would clip each thread from bottom to top to keep the chaps tight.

There came a time when I was proficient enough to move 20 or 30 head of cattle all by myself with a couple of cow dogs. The drive was about 10 to 15 miles down the road from the RO to the Wineglass Ranch, where the cattle could graze on the wild grass in the larger pastures. Herding the cows meant keeping the mother cows with their calves and not letting them stray or run away. I must keep them together. Now my horse was no longer that gentle old nag I learned on, but rather a jumpy mustang requiring strict control. I sat firmly in the saddle so that the horse knew who was in charge. There was always a need to be alert and on the lookout for him to kick or buck. Over the years, I knew I was gaining respect from the other cowboys because of their comments. They didn't give out many compliments, but when they did, they meant it. It took many 12- to 14-hour days moving cows in the blistering sun or the frost-bitten winter wind. Yet, my enduring love for open spaces, crystal-clear air, mountain streams, and the quiet splendor of riding alone at sunrise or sunset always drew me back.

Some of the dangers I faced gave me an adrenaline rush. For example, a steer might try to gore my horse. I had to keep my distance but still maintaining the pressure on the steer until he is corralled. The large bull would charge, unafraid of the horse, so I had to stay on the horse as he ran and bucked. Sometimes a couple of cowboys would have to rope a bull and pull him into the corral. I spent many a day chasing a calf across the desert and down a steep ravine, my horse nearly stumbling. Yes, I would occasionally get bucked off, but all I could do was get up, brush off, and mount again, and carry on…COWBOY UP.

Ed began to give me more spirited horses to ride and work the cattle. Though only half-broken, these native Mustangs could outwork and outlast the thoroughbreds.

The long work days from sunrise to sundown clearly were hard, but the joy of being on the boundless prairie, under the startling, big, blue skies, made up for it. Often it was just my horse and me, moving a few head of cattle here and there. Sometimes it was so quiet I could hear a lizard scurry off in front of me. The fresh scent of the blooming sage and the glorious colors of its blossoms always took my breath away.

In the evenings, Ed would show me several ways to weave together strips of leather for a horsewhip or a fancy rein for my bridle. He would tell me stories of his early cowboy days and the various ranches he worked on over the years. He described the dangers, and the pleasures, of working with cows. Now that he is gone, I often think of those stories, especially when I am traveling through some of the areas where we moved cows together. Ed's wife, Ella, also taught me some great tips for cooking on a cattle ranch — how to preserve meat, and vegetables, and how to store milk in the basement so the cream would rise to the top to make butter. She was so kind, always having a fresh pair of Levis ready for me each morning as I headed to breakfast. I often stayed in their spare bedroom when working on the ranch. I am sorrowful that they are gone, yet the fond memories bring joy to my life.

When I began learning to fly a helicopter, I noticed the similarities to my work on the ranch -- repeating each movement over and over, exactly like when Ed taught me to ride. "Take care of your aircraft and it will take care of you." That was just like Ed vigorously reminding me, "Take care of your horse and your horse will take care of you!"

Everything I remember about the ranch blends with the lessons I learned as a combat pilot, be it dealing with the other pilots and gunners, helping with maintenance, or working with the aircraft. It was not unlike helping the other cowboys with their horses when they were too tired or lazy to cool them down at the end of the day correctly.

The pattern was repeated when I worked closely with court clerks, court reporters, and judges. All relationships depended on my ability to work collaboratively. Respect all those working around you, and they will extend the same to you. Often, I would be the first one called to the front of the line to file my pleadings or get the copy of the transcript because of the rapport I had built with the staff. I developed lasting and respectful relationships with fellow lawyers — even with the prosecutors when I was a defense attorney.

# COWBOY STORIES

When I did not have to care for the horses in the early morning, I would sleep in a little extra. Then grab my Levies, shirt, boots and run to the cook house. Quickly wash my hands and face in the bowl on the back porch, anxiously awaiting morning breakfast, which was usually grand, always— steak, eggs, biscuits and gravy, potatoes, and fresh milk. But the best part of any meal, whether in the clean cookhouse or around the campfire on a trail, was listening to the cowboys tell stories of their adventures.

 I recall some of the great stories of the "real" cowboys and the inimitable comments of the cowhands. This one, I was actually involved with, it is the typical short but sweet truth:

*************************

*When finishing our day of rounding up cows, I saw, near sunset, a cowboy riding hard, chasing a Young fast heifer. The cowboy returned to camp without the heifer. I asked what had happened, why no heifer? The cowboy, made a single simple statement: "The further I pursued her, the dimmer she got."*

I also recall one old cowhand could tell a tale; I remember one remarkable story:

*************************

*In the early twenties, when I first left home at 15 years of age, my parents gave me a horse, a pack mule, and a couple of bags of clothes and stuff. Just before sunset, after ridin' all day on my way from Arizona to Nevada, I spotted a campfire. I saw four cowboys sittin' around the fire and about half a dozen cows penned up in a sagebrush corral at the edge of the camp. One of the men asked, "Do you wanna join us? Have a cuppa hot coffee and stay the night." I took 'em up on their offer. After finishin' the coffee, I took my horse and pack mule to the edge of camp. I shackled the two of 'em, then pulled the saddle off my horse and my bags off the pack mule.*

*As I was fixin' my sleepin' gear on the ground, another cowboy, not from the camp, came up to me. This man was packin' a "six-gun." I thought it was a little strange that he positioned himself so that the four cowboys at the camp couldn't see him. He asked me, "Did you just join the others around the fire?"*

*"Yes," I said, "I'm ridin' from Arizona on my way to Nevada."*

*"You might want to leave early in the mornin' before the cowhands get up," he warned. Then he rode off.*

***********************

As the storyteller paused, everyone at the breakfast table waited intently to hear what happened next. The cowboy related that he heeded the advice; before sunrise, he gathered his horse and pack mule and quietly headed down the trail while the four cowboys were still asleep. However, curiosity got the best of him, so he doubled around and headed back to the camp.

***********************

*When I got back, I saw all four of them cowboys with their hands tied behind their backs, strung up by the neck in a hangman's noose, danglin' from the nearest trees! The cowboy with the six-gun, who warned me to leave early, was gatherin' up the cows along with five other cowboys. I found out they were local ranch owners and had lynched the four cowboys at the camp for bein' cattle rustlers."*

***********************

As the old cowboy at the breakfast table finished the story, I saw tears in his eyes.

***********************

I heard other remarkable stories over breakfast, dinner, or supper — or maybe around the campfire.

One cowboy started by explaining how there had been conflicts between the cattlemen and the sheepherders back in the thirties and forties in rural Nevada. When I asked why there were conflicts, the cowboy looked startled, as though I should have known.

*************************

*When the sheep come across the open range, they eat all the prairie grass down so short that the grass won't re-seed and will burn out in the hot summer months, preventin' any growth in the followin' year. The ground just becomes a dustbowl. Since the sheep are just passin' through, they don't care about the land. Cows, on the other hand, are much smarter animals and don't eat the prairie grass all the way down to the roots. That means the grass will still seed and grow every spring.*

*************************

The storyteller indicated that his story was about the cattle and sheep wars. It was not something that involved him; a lawyer from Reno had told him about the incident.

*************************

*This lawyer told me he used to help any cowboy who was down on his luck. He helped one old cowboy by giving him some money to go back to Oklahoma to die. The lawyer asked that down-and-out cowhand if he had anything to trade in exchange for the money. The cowboy said, "I got sump'n, but there's a story behind it."*

*The old cowboy told him that in the late twenties and early thirties, the local cattlemen ranchers with "open-range" grazing rights hired gunfighters to run off the sheepherders. This cowboy was one of them gunfighters and killed four or five sheepherders. He shot a lot of their sheep, too.*

*The old gunfighter said, "They finally caught up with me and tried me for murder. I was found guilty and sentenced to die by hangin'. The hangin' was gonna be at the garrison at Fort Churchill, out of Virginia City. On the day of the hangin', they led me up the stairs to the gallows. They pulled the noose tight around my neck, and put a black silk hangman's bag over my head. Just before they were gonna give the signal to pull the trap door, the governor of the state of Nevada, who was an old cattleman himself, rode into the fort and immediately pardoned me! They took off the noose, untied my hands, and I pulled that black hood off from over my head. The governor gave me a horse, told me I was free, and told me to git outta town."*

*As he told this story to the lawyer, the old cowboy reached in his back pocket. He pulled out a black silk hangman's bag — the one that had been pulled over his head. This was all he had of any value. The lawyer gave him the money to go back to Oklahoma and told him to keep the hangman's bag.*

***********************

My uncle also told me a real story at the breakfast table that happened when he first bought the RO.

***********************

*When I first took over the RO, I had some old lifelong cowboys working for me that had been cowboy'n for 20 to 25 years. Most had never married. I would pay them once a month in cash. They would hitch a ride into Tonopah on Friday night. They would be gone maybe 2 or three days. Most would put their money in a sack and hand it to the bartender, drink until it was gone, saving'n a little to stop at Boddie's Buckeye bar, a brothel, before catching a ride back to the ranch. Sometimes they would buy a new pair of Levi's and white shirt for a Saturday night dance. But that was their monthly entertainment.*

***********************

Carl went on telling another story:

*"This one old salt was helpin' vaccinate some cows in the pen. One stepped on his big toe real hard. He was hobblin' around; couldn't even go into town. So, one evening he got drunk, took out his Winchester 30/30, pulled off his boot, and shot his toe off! I don't have to tell ya', we rushed him to the hospital in Tonopah. After losin' a toe, he actually had to learn how to walk again.*

***********************

Before I started staying in Ed and Ella Fishers' spare room, I slept in the one-room shack shared by all the cowhands. There was nothing except cots with footlockers at the ends. A nail on the wall was for hanging hats. Couple of tables and chairs to play cards, and a pot belly stove. There were no interior bathrooms, only the outhouse. No running water. The few cowboys who bathed did so on Saturdays at the cook shack. Sometimes the cowboys would pay Ella to wash their clothes, but most never did, nor did they change their long johns.

To be more percise, there is one constant about the bunkhouse that made it instantly recognizable: the smell. The aroma that assaulted the senes of anyone walking in was a composite of sweaty men sleeping in "long-johns" that had never been washed, dry cow manure caked on their boots, the licorice in chewing-tabacco plugs, and the smoke from lamps that were burning kerosene oil when the electricity went out. But the true cowhand never complained they were usually loaners, and didn't talk much.

## THE ELEMENTS AND WATER

In the mountains and valleys of Nevada, a cattle rancher needs to know where the grazing is best. During the winter, the desert flatlands present a surprising abundance of feed, be it the wild grass growing around sagebrush, the blossoms of the sagebrush themselves, or the bushes. There is much less snow and cold in the lowlands than in the mountains, so in winter, the cattle would graze on the plains. In the summer months, the animals are moved into the hills, where there are streams and meadow grass.

The problem in Nevada is that if the cows are in the desert flatlands, there are very few, if any, streams or watersheds. The water must be kept in open troughs, and the only source to fill them is deep-water wells. There are no power lines to run an electric pump.

Then came the windmill. This marvelous machine, driven by the wind and equipped with vanes or sails, pulls the water several hundred feet out of the ground and pours it into the water trough. Typically, windmills and water troughs are placed several miles apart throughout the winter grazing area.

Each winter morning, a cowboy must rise before sunrise to saddle up and ride to each sector to verify that the windmill is working and that the water is not frozen. Sometimes a small gas engine is needed to pump the water. (This device never starts when you pull on the starting rope — at least, not until your arms are tired.) Sometimes, if the old 1940s pickup truck will turn over and start, the cowboy can travel to some of the areas by vehicle and even take hay to supplement the feed. That is, if there is not a blinding snowstorm and the cows have not scattered. Usually, the vehicle fails to start anyway, or the bald tires are flat, so the cowboy goes by horseback.

If it is summer, the cowboy doesn't have to worry about water because the creek provides plenty of it in the mountains. He does have to keep rattlesnakes, bobcats, or mountain lions away from the cows, and ensure that the makeshift camp has plenty of wood so that the cook can prepare meals in the wood stove or over the campfire.

The rule of thumb is that it takes two or three acres of grazing land to feed one cow. That is tough to provide in the dry desert land of central Nevada. Some summers are extremely wet while the cows are in the mountains. Then, in the winter months, there will be a lot of sagebrushes, grass around the bushes, and blooms on the sagebrush. The watering troughs are sometimes 10 or 15 miles apart. The cattle spread out all over the flat.

It is quite a sight to see how the cows work with each other to graze and drink. I was on the flat one cold winter, moving cows around or bringing them supplemental hay. We had set up a little camp and were building a campfire and getting some grub together. I looked up and saw all the mother cows heading to the nearest water hole, maybe four or five miles across the flat. Their calves remained in one area with an old bull. It was as if the bull had been left to keep watch over the calves. When the mother cows returned a few hours later and the calves started suckling, the old bull walked to the waterhole by himself. I could not determine their means of communication. It was just decisive, collaborative, remarkable action.

The elements are not only hard on the cattle and calves, but also on the cowboy and horses. The temperature ranges between 80 and 120 degrees Fahrenheit in the summer, and as low as 30 degrees below zero in the winter, depending on the wind.

Then, of course, there are the snowstorms and whiteouts during the winter on the flatlands. We cowboys would round up the cattle and corral them in the fenced areas of the home ranch so that we could feed them hay when the winter was very hard and the food scarce. But the task was not easy. First of all, back in the 1950s and 1960s, we had no lightweight thermal gear to wear. All we could do was layer our shirts, coats, and Levis. Then it was hard to get on the horse. I was very short until I turned 14, and the horse was very tall, so often I had to find a boulder to climb on while keeping the horse close enough that I could swing aboard.

Trying to get on my horse was quite a challenge, especially in parts of the desert flat where there were few boulders. Sometimes I would jump on a big bush on top of a sand dune. It would often take several tries, but I persisted. I also learned how to hold my bladder for a long time so that I could remain on the horse as long as possible.

How clearly I recall when I got caught in a whiteout while trying to move cows. I was with Eddie Sherin, here  roll'n his own,

a seasoned cowboy and close friend. We were driving cows about 15 miles down the mountain from Tonopah. We had gathered them from the flat and were planning to corral them in the holding pens at Miller's, the closest well with a corral. We could give them some salt and hay, and maybe load them on our only cattle truck to take them to the RO. We had rounded up about 100 head and were a couple of miles from the fenced area at Miller's when a blizzard hit us. The light snow became a treacherous gale. The wind blew at 20 to 30 miles an hour, and visibility was near zero. We couldn't see more than two feet in front of us. The cows started scattering, but we could not see well enough to keep them together, nor could we tell what direction we were heading. With the wind and snow, we could not even hear the stock move.

What to do? Tonopah was about 15 miles away. If we followed the paved road, we could get ourselves and our horses warmed up by riding through the open sliding doors at the Chevron garage. We had done that a few times before, but which way was Tonopah? I was only about 13 or 14, and I was getting scared. Eddie sensed my fear and said, "Let's start galloping our horses along the side of the paved road. Follow me."

I had no idea which direction we were going. It would be Tonopah in 14 miles or Coaldale in 30 miles. I followed

Eddie's horse as fast and as close as visibility would allow. Then Eddie stopped and said, "Tonopah is this way."

"How in the hell do you know that?"

"Look at the horses. They are breathing hard. They are straining as they run. That means they are running uphill. That is the way to Tonopah. If we were running downhill, they would not be breathing so hard, and would not have been working so hard to move."

What a lesson! An old cowboy who only finished eighth grade, but he knew how to survive. The only way to learn something like that is to have the experience — or read this book.

The summers posed another problem. When I had to round up the cattle to do branding, or take them to a corral to load them onto trucks for moving or selling, it was hard to make progress in the heat of the day. Not only was it hard on horse and rider, but also dangerous for the cattle. Therefore, most work was done in the early morning hours. We quit at midday, but we would be back at it about four or five, usually completing the work just before sunset.

Indian summer in Nevada is the most enjoyable time to be a cowboy! Indian summer starts in September and ends in November. It isn't quite winter or summer. Cold, crisp mornings, cool, still nights — the cowhand's dream. Riding out together with the herd in the quiet morning is invigorating. The nights are just chilly enough to require a good-sized blanket, but are not freezing. How often we would sit around the campfire, listening to the cowboy stories, or relax and quietly admire the beauty of the stars and night air.

But then, all too soon, came winter. Getting water to the cattle during the winter months on the frozen flatlands became more and more involved. The windmills had old black grease that would freeze, and the wind vanes would not turn, nor would the pumping system pull the water from the deep well. A few of the old hand pumps might work once in a while — but then came the gasoline engines.

I invented new and extremely harsh cuss words for those mechanical devices. The principle was straightforward. First, make sure the fuel tank is full of gas and on. Adjust the spark and slightly pull out the choke. Make sure the belt to the pump is tight so that when the engine starts, the pump will pull the water from the deep well. Gently pull the start cord and this incredible engine will magically start.

That was what the brochure said — but remember, these engines were made in the 1940s. No one performed any maintenance on them at all. Occasionally a little box was built around the machines, but more often than not they were left out in the elements. Each cowboy had their technique to adjusting the spark just right and pulling the choke correctly without flooding the carburetor, and jerking on the starter cord when we each took our turn at starting it.

An additional issue in using this exact science was that we had to rely on our wits after moving cattle several miles in freezing weather, or in the summers when we moved the cows from the flat to the highlands; some days were over 120 degrees. We were all tired, including the horses. The cattle were thirsty, and there was no water in the trough. One cowboy after another took his turn getting the pump going. Finally, the fresh, cold water would flow out of the pipe to be enjoyed by all, man and beast.

During wartime, I recall hiding at the edge of the jungle, waiting for a rescue craft to pick up my gunner and me. Fighting with the gas engine to pump the water would fill my mind, replace my fears when I was in danger making jungle predicament less stressful.

One particular time, my gunner and I were laying down hiding in a rice paddy away from enemy machine gun fire while our gunships were taking out the enemy position so the rescue ship could pick us up. I looked down at my flight gloves and for an instant, I thought about when I left my gloves at the cook shack and got bucked off my horse to get the gloves, and slammed to the ground. The stress of the situation was completely erased for an instant.

## POOR SETTLERS IN EARLY NEVADA

Most of the small ranches that Carl bought in the fifties and sixties had been developed by poor settlers. Also called homesteaders because they obtained the land under the Homestead Act signed by President Abraham Lincoln on May 20, 1862. The main ranch, RO, was a massive spread, but these homesteaders had only about 160 acres with a 12 X 14 dwelling, well, windmill, barn, corral, and often an orchard – Oh, we cannot forget the outhouse.

As a young cowboy, I would go to the smaller spreads to gather cattle or cut and bale the grass in the meadows. I was always intrigued by how the corrals and the barn had been developed by a homesteader. All these improvements were almost identical. Carl did improve some of the old houses by building a water tank, filled by the windmill.

The water was piped to the kitchen sink for cooking and washing, but the toilets remained the same – the outhouse. Almost every one of the homes on these small ranches had a potbelly stove. A potbelly stove is a cast-iron, wood-burning stove, round with a bulge in the middle — hence the name. If you have never used one, you would be in for a treat. Often, I was required to be the first up each morning to build the fire in the potbelly stove, usually for brewing coffee.

I'd stumble around in the dark, looking for a match to light a candle or lantern. It took some effort to start the fire. You could not just put paper under wood; that did not guarantee the fire would start. After filling the house with smoke several times, I learned first to make sure the draft was open, then crumple paper and stick it a little way up the stovepipe.

I would crumple more paper in the stove, then cut small pieces of wood, and place them on top of the torn sheets of paper. I would light the paper in the stovepipe first, then the paper with the pieces of wood on top in the main part of the stove. The burning paper in the stovepipe would cause the air to go up the pipe and draw the flame. As the small pieces of wood ignited, I would add larger wood, or even coal if that was available. Finally, I would smell that pleasant odor of burning embers. If the room was still dark, I could see the fire from the cracks in the stove and hear the crackling of the sap if the wood was pine. My next step would be to fill the coffee pot, pour in and let it boil — cowboy coffee latte. Carl did have a few kitchen stoves and ovens, but these initially used wood as well.

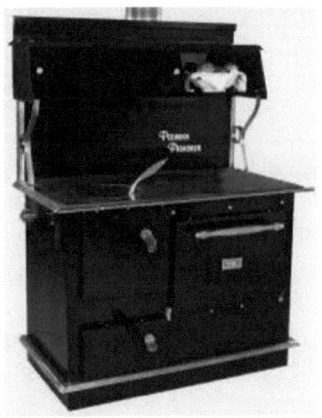

However, by the time I started working at those outer ranches, Carl had replaced the old wood-burning ovens with new gas-burning stoves and ovens.

Most spreads also had a nice little creek running through the meadows. The stream was perfect for fishing and even bathing, though the latter activity was never performed by the old cowboys. The early homesteaders designed their homes or storage rooms so that the stream or creek water would run through them and provide a cooling system for the hot summers. They might divert some of the water from the creek to a little orchard to keep the fruit trees alive and producing. These small ranches were so quiet that you would swear you could hear a rabbit hopping by — except when you were being entertained by the cricket orchestra along with the creek.

All these smaller ranches still used outhouses. A toilet that usually needs some fresh white lye spread in the hole. The distinctive smell of the outhouses lingers in my memories. It took a lot of getting used to, especially when there was no fresh lye to kill the smell. One quickly learned to go in, rapidly get his business done, and exit. No reading the morning paper or a favorite magazine.

Almost every outhouse looked the same: wooden walls and seat with a round hole in the middle. The wood was usually gray from age, and the wooden boards making up the walls had shrunk, so there were small spaces between the boards where the cold air would leak through. The seat was usually worn down slick, so there wasn't a worry about getting splinters in your backside. Still, you had to sit just right because if you got off the flat part, a sticker or two was guaranteed.

Every door seemed to squeak the exact same way when opening and closing. The hinges were always rusty, and one or two had rusted all the way through. Sometimes the door might be hanging on by only one hinge. The real treat, however, was trying to use an outhouse in the dark of night. It didn't take long before a little kerosene lamp accompanied me to the outhouse.

The main ranch at the RO was more living-friendly than the smaller outer ranches. Carl's main house, where I often stayed when I was young, had three bedrooms and indoor bathrooms. It even had a shower. The cook shack was a large building with a couple of rooms for the cook and family, as well as a large table for the cowhands. The early days of a washroom with a hand water pump gave way to a bathroom with full plumbing. There was a large bunkhouse for the cowhands and, of course, an outhouse.

There was a large fenced corral and a barn

with a separate tack room for hanging saddles, bridles, horse blankets, and pads, as well as spare lariats.

The tack room was also where the grain bags were stored, as well as a fifty-gallon barrel of wheat with which to fill the bags. There was no lighting, so I usually stumbled around in the dark if I had to fill the grain sacks before breakfast. On one occasion, I reached into the grain barrel to get the scoop and grabbed ahold of a giant snake. Needless to say, I was lucky it was only a bull snake. There were a lot of rattlesnakes

in central Nevada, and it could just as easily have been one of them.

After that experience, I made it very clear that if there was to be any filling of the sack before daylight, it was not going to be by me. I wouldn't even go back into the barn for several days because the event had scared me so much.

Every area of the ranch had its own character. The central cookhouse had a metal triangle dinner bell hanging loose on a chain.

The chef would take a metal rod and ring the triangle to announce breakfast, supper, and dinner. We would all head to the back door, where we would fill the wash pan and clean our hands and faces.

The tack room next to the barn was chock full of equipment. All the saddles hung from ropes strung over the rafters

or were mounted on wooden sawhorses.

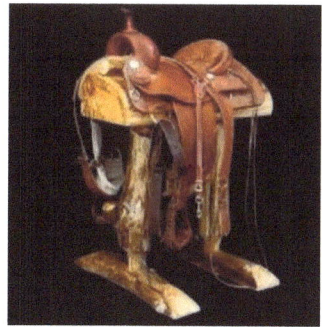

The bridles and lariats dangled from large nails on the walls.

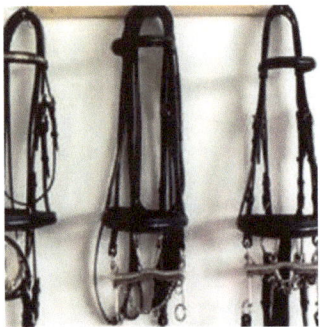

The Lariats were close at hand when riding to catch that little calf that decides to run off.

The saddle blanket and pad would keep the horse' back from getting raw from the saddle rubbing. Pad first then blanket.

There were tools and supplies to repair stirrups, reins, and most anything else related to the horses. My additional chores included ensuring this room was always clean, with everything in its place.

There were tools and supplies to repair stirrups, reins, and most anything else related to the horses. My additional chores included ensuring this room was always clean, with everything in place.

The strong smell of leather still lingers in my mind. I do not know why leather is so appealing, but when I go into a store selling leather briefcases or coats, the memories of cleaning the tack room instantly flash forward.

# RANCH WORK

On a small central Nevada cattle ranch, the cowhand doesn't just work with cows like in the movies. Other chores include cutting, baling, and stacking hay; fixing fences; being a mechanic, plumber, electrician, carpenter, welder, and leatherworker; and, of course, mucking the shit out of the barn. In the early days of sailing ships, animal manure would sometimes get wet, ferment, and release explosive methane gas while being transported. Many an unsuspecting sailor stumbled below decks with a candle or lantern, causing a fire and maybe even sinking the vessel. The captains learned to write on the sacks of manure, "Ship High in Transit," or just "SHIT." The term survives to this day.

A real cowpoke will take care of his horse and treat cows humanely. However, the mechanic is the indispensable person on the modern ranch. He must be strong, determined, resourceful, and a jack of all trades. The mechanic literally keeps everything running. He must know the old equipment, new equipment, and how to combine the two. During my early visits and later as a worker at the RO Ranch, Gene Daniels was a master mechanic and a genius in the garage. Gene had been at the ranch forever.

Gene didn't have much to do with me when I was growing up. He was a quiet man; he just wanted to be left alone to do his job. Gene was tall and a little hunched over, probably from leaning over engines for so many years. His hands were the size of flapjacks and as hard as steel. His fingers were yellow from smoking and rolling his own cigarettes. He had dark piercing eyes, well-earned wrinkles, and short, dirty hair. He always wore a greasy cap and, of course, overalls that were covered with grease, oil, or hydraulic fluid.

As I got older, my uncle Carl allowed me to work in the garage with Gene and have him teach me a few simple things, like changing oil, filling batteries, and fixing tires. Later, I even got to work on fuel pumps and carburetors. Gene once let me help him break down an engine to rebuild. He taught me how to fix the hay baler if the wiring mechanism was busted. I even learned how to sharpen and adjust the blades of the sickle, swather, and combine.

Gene would not let me get away with anything. I had to hand him the right tool, the right bolt, or the right nut as soon as he asked for one. When I was wrong, he would complain, "How many times must I tell you?" as he rolled from under the truck or tracker, mad as a hornet.

Sadly, toward the end of my time working on the ranch, I had to fly Gene in my uncle's plane to San Francisco for cancer treatment. He hated being a burden. He once told me on the way back home that he did not want to waste away. One early morning, my uncle went to check on him and found that he had killed himself with his six gun. Knowing Gene as we did, we figured that no doubt that was how he wanted to go. Though he never socialized with the other workers, when he smiled it came from his heart. He was a warm and kind man, missed by all.

What is a Central Nevada ranch going to do without a work truck? These vehicles were usually old and broken, but they did the job of getting us around, hauling hay and an occasional cow or calf. I learned to drive a 1956 Chevy flatbed with a four-speed stick shift. I had a heck of a time getting the clutch all the way down because of my short legs, but I learned. The knob on the gearshift was broken in half, so when I forgot my gloves, I got cuts and bruises from using it. The flatbed was made of old hardwood, and because of its age it was gray in color. If I wasn't careful when loading bales of hay, one of the boards could break, and I could fall through. If I didn't have gloves, I could count on getting at least one splinter. If that happened, of course, I had to keep working, and my whole hand would get infected and swollen. I would have to cut the abscess open with my knife so that the pus could drain out.

I would soon learn how to add new wooden boards and fix all the tires, the fuel pump, and the carburetor. I would even blow into the gas tank when the old engine vapor locked. We would take the broken side boards off when using the truck to stack bales, then put them back on when moving a cow or calves. The old leather seats were dirty black, not the nice tan they were when new. The saddle blanket, tied with baling wire, kept the seats cool so that I could sit on them in the sunshine. Finally, there had to be a burlap water bag hanging from the front of the truck tied to the Chevy logo on the hood. This water bag is a simple but marvelous invention. The water would seep slowly through the burlap and evaporate in the heat. That evaporation cooled, keeping the water as fresh as any of today's expensive water bottles!

When I first started haying with the old flatbed, the hay crew consisted of a driver, one man walking on the ground to throw the bales, and a man standing on the flatbed to catch them. The bales usually had two strains of wire weighing 40 to 50 pounds. The man on the flatbed would grab the bales with his hay hook, drag them to the truck, and stack them as high as he could, maybe two or three rows up. Finally, my cheap uncle purchased a simple slide loader — a long metal slide that had a chain with teeth running up the middle and wheels on each side, connected to the side of the truck. As the wheels turned, the chain worked on a pulley so that the driver could capture the bale on the ground. He would scoop it up and the teeth would grab it and move it up the slide. As the bale ran up the ramp, the man on the deck waited until it was high enough, then grabbed it with the hay hook, bounced it off his knees, and thrust it into place. There was no longer a need for someone to toss the bale from the ground to the stacker. It made the work easier, but because of the automation, one man lost his job.

Aside from the ranch truck and the tractors for farming, the Mustang was the most frequently used mode of transportation on the ranches. The Mustang is a free-roaming horse of the American West descended from horses brought to the Americas by the Spanish. Mustangs are often referred to as wild horses, but because they are descended from once-domesticated horses, they are more accurately defined as feral animals. The original Mustangs were from Spain, but many other breeds and types of horses contributed to the modern Mustang's bloodline, resulting in varying phenotypes. Free-roaming horse herds vary in the degree to which they can be traced to the original

Iberian horses. Some contain a mixture of breeds, usually from ranch stock released for various reasons. Others are relatively unchanged from the original Iberian stock.

Though my uncle and a few of the older cowhands had their own purebreds, like Tennessee Walkers, the other hands and I were given Mustangs. Most of these horses were only partially broken. This meant that after the fight to get the bridle, saddle blanket, and saddle on the horse, he would always try to buck me off when I mounted — especially early on a cold morning.

I learned to grab a handful of mane while grabbing the horn and swinging on, making sure the cinch was very tight. Sometimes I would have to get a little mean if the beast was being mean himself. Along with grabbing the mane, I might have to poke the horse in the eye or kick him in the leg, or twist his ear — anything to get his mind off trying to buck me off. It often seemed that the horse knew that once I was in the saddle, we were both looking at a ten- to twelve-hour workday pushing cows.

Real ranch work means fighting with the horse. It means fighting to get the old tractor to start so the cowhand can fill the water trough or fix the hay baler. It may mean sharpening and tightening the blades on the sickle to cut the hay for baling. It's struggling with the spools of baling wire to be loaded on the flatbed when mending fences. In short, there is nothing glorious about being a cowboy and working on a cattle ranch in the hot summer or cold winter — except for the stunning natural beauty of the land, which always brings the cowboys back!

The radiance of the golden sunrise or sunset, or the night sky with stars sparkling like diamonds, always made me forget my difficulties. The stars looked close enough for me to grab them. Then there was the beauty of the harvest moon. I could swear it was smiling down on me. Remembering the stillness of the night while circling the cows on cattle drives still sends chills down my spine.

The cow boss told me about something that had happened in the 1950s. In those days, the only way to get all the supplies and materials to a high camp where the cows did their summer grazing was to use pack animals. The horses or mules would be loaded with food, grain, and other essentials. The lead cowboy would guide his horse or mule with a lead rope. The next in line would have his lead rope tied to the tail of the horse in front. The line amounted to as many as 10 animals and often sets of two or three. The caravan would follow the trail along the creek to the high camp. It was done at a slow pace, and usually there was no difficulty except for when an occasional rattlesnake spooked the horses.

Once at camp, we unloaded and corralled the animals. The high camp had a barn and a cook shack. There was a place for a campfire and an area outside where the cowboys slept and stored their gear. The camp was 10 to 12 miles up the mountain from the RO.

We put hay in the wooden trough for the horses' evening meal. However, in the early morning we used feed bags just as we did at the home ranch. The cowboy had to go to the corral with all the horses and place the bags over their heads, let them eat, and then remove the bags.

On one occasion, an old cowhand named Barnie Mainer had the early morning job. There were between 10 and 15 animals to feed. All the bags were filled with fresh seed. Barnie headed to the corral, but apparently the animals started fighting, kicking, and biting. Barnie got kicked, went down, and was trampled. Bleeding like a stuck pig, he managed to crawl to the side of the corral and squeeze under the fence. Luckily, the cow boss spotted him, and a couple of hands helped carry Barnie to the cook shack. In those days, cowboys didn't have first-aid kits, but they tried their best to patch him up. They knew that Barnie might die if he wasn't taken to the hospital.

It was the cow boss' responsibility to get him there, so he loaded Barnie belly down on a pack horse, tying his arms and feet together under the stomach of the animal. The cow boss mounted his own horse, grabbed the reins of the pack horse carrying Barnie, and started down the mountain.

Though Barnie was still bleeding, in addition to being bandaged, dirty, and hurt, the cow boss found a chance to play a prank. There were several fishermen ahead of them along the creek trail. Knowing they were probably from California, he wanted to give the "prune pickers" something to talk about when they returned home. He reached to the holster holding his trusty Winchester 30/30 – which we all carried to fend off coyotes, mountain lions, and bobcats – and laid it across his lap. He didn't look at any of the fishermen. He just stared straight ahead, slowly leading Barney through their camp. What a spectacle it must have been — a rough-and-ready cowboy, with a rifle on his lap and a bleeding man tied to a pack animal behind. I'm sure they all thought the sheriff had gotten his man!

Nevertheless, Barnie's accident was a reminder that animals are unpredictable and can be dangerous. Later, I realized how my habit of being aware of my surroundings would save my life in combat situations.

I also learned to take care of my equipment. We all used the standard bridle to control the horse. This device is a harness-type leather strap with metal rings and a metal bit that slips into the horse's mouth. It is designed to pull the horse's jaw up when pulled directly back. This causes the horse to stop. A chin strap holds the bridle on the head, with the top being tightened over the head. The reins run along each side of the horse's neck. There is also a bridle called a "hackamore," which is more comfortable for the animal. A hackamore does not have a bit. Instead, it has a noseband that works on pressure points on the face, nose, and chin. It takes lots of training to get the horse to obey commands when wearing this device.

The modern western saddle begins with a "tree" that defines the shape of the bars, the seat, the swells, the horn, and the cantle. Traditional trees are made of wood covered with rawhide and coated with varnish or a similar synthetic coating. A real cowhand will oil his saddle often to keep it from drying out and becoming brittle.

Starting the day meant knowing what could happen if one did not stay alert and prepared. That also meant remembering to bring all one's gear. I recall an incident that caused me great pain. One morning after getting saddled up, I realized that I had left my gloves in the cook shack, so I rode over to the front of the shack. While I climbed off the horse, a cow dog ran under him. The horse spooked and jumped back. My foot got stuck in a stirrup. To keep from getting dragged, I let go of the saddle horn and grabbed my stuck boot with both hands to jerk it out of the stirrup. Of course, that meant I had no way to hold on. I got slammed flat on my back and onto the hard ground. I was laid up for more than a week.

Another accident happened because I was careless. I had been working with an old International Harvester backhoe, and the fuel pump bulb got clogged. I knew how to unhook the bulb and clean out the debris. I should have used a jack to lift the tractor, and then placed a wood block under it to get to the gas pump safely. Instead, I simply used the front loader to lift the front of the backhoe. I then crawled under the tractor to see about taking the lamp apart. In less than a heartbeat, I heard a slight crack. To this day, I don't know what made me react, but in that split second, I pulled myself from under the backhoe. As my leg cleared the front end, the loader gave way and the tractor slammed to the ground. Had I not moved in time, I would have been crushed! Like so many other lessons, this instinctive reaction also would serve me well in combat.

Trust and collaboration are critical for cowhands. I recall one time when a big old bull got into a large bush and refused to back out. One of the cowhands on horseback roped him and tried to pull him out. A second cowboy got off his horse to push the mad bull out of the bush. The bull lunged at the cowhand on the ground, but the cowboy on horseback reared back, pulling the rope tightly enough to jerk the large animal onto its side. He saved the cowboy on the ground from being gored. The cowboy knew that the other man had his back, and that was why he got off his horse.

The same confidence that we cowboys had each other's backs was established among my comrades in arms. As a combat scout, my job was to fly "nap of the earth" to find enemy soldiers. This meant I would take fire most every time I found the enemy. However, I knew the gunship pilots would stay alert; once I yelled "taking fire!" they would gun down whoever was targeting me.

I cannot tell about working on the ranch without mentioning my job sewing sacks on a Messy Harris Combine. The machine was pulled by a farm tractor. The front of the machine had a cutting blade or sickle. These blades cut the heads off the wheat, and the heads fell into the trough onto a moving belt. The grain was sifted through different screens with the wheat pouring through one of the three open binds. One of the workers would lift each sack up and down, hooked to each bind to fill the bag. Once full, he would hand it to me.

When I had the full sack, I would sew it shut using a needle that looked like an arrowhead with a metal link at the other end. I would use a little half-hitch on one ear, then a couple of stitches, then another half-hitch. Once tied, out the back went the sack to be picked up by the crew on the ground. The wheat chaff consisted of the husks of corn or other seeds separated by winnowing or threshing. Chaff filled the cabin or packing compartment of the machine so thickly that we could almost cut it with a knife. We would wear goggles to keep our eyes from getting infected. The chaff even got deep into my clothes. Sometimes when I wore the same T-shirts a year later, they still had pieces of chaff in them.

An old cowboy named Red once took a turn packing the sacks. This meant standing and stamping each sack from each separate open bend, then handing the full bag to the sewer. But poor old Red had broken his nose so many times, there was not a set of goggles that he could wear to keep the chaff out of his eyes. He lasted only two days on the job before he quit.

Then there was the time I stabbed myself in the hand with the arrowhead needle. Eddie Sherin, the driver of the tractor pulling the machine, thought it was hilarious because I squealed like a stuck pig. I got mad and said, "OK, you SOB, sitting up front in the fresh open air, it's your turn to get off that nice cushy driving seat and get back in the sacking hell room filled with chaff." Thus, Eddie Sherin the driver became Eddie Sherin the sack-sewer. But without Eddie noticing, I slipped from second gear to third gear. The bags began filling up much faster, and Eddie was having a hard time keeping up. Oh, sweet revenge! Eddie stabbed himself in the hand with the needle and squawked even louder than I had. The whole crew had to stop and take a break because no one could stop laughing.

That was a typical day of hard work — we just tried to make it fun. We would even draw funny faces on the sacks and write the name of Burt Ramos, head of the ground crew, on them. Before throwing them to the ground, Burt and his team would laugh, load the sacks, and move them to the barn for feed in the winter.

# MOVING COWS

Why is it that, when you are on horseback on the open prairie, even during the warm summer months, the air seems so crisp and cool just as the golden sun rises, even more than it does before sunrise? Anyone who has had the opportunity to experience this phenomenon will agree with the truth of such an unusual manifestation. The air is also filled with the astonishing, exhilarating fragrance of blooming sagebrush, which flaunts rainbow colors as far as the eye can see — that is, if there had been a really wet winter.

As the sky melts from the deep golden stillness of sunrise to vivid ocean blue, day breaks. The morning dew covering the ground and the sagebrush slowly evaporates. It is as if the sagebrush is taking one last drink of water before facing the scorching summer sun. This is how I remember the mornings when we were to move cattle from the flat land of the desert to the high mountain meadows of Twin Rivers, about fifteen miles up the canyon from the RO Ranch.

The cattle drives were arduous in the summer. Blowing dust storms, or "dust devils," scattered the herd. The cowboys had to chase down the cows and bring them back...provided that we could see. Most of the time the sand was so thick, I could see only a couple of feet in front of me. When that happened, we would often lose the cows because they would take off back to their favorite water hole, where we had started gathering them two days earlier.

When moving cows, we worked sun up to sundown. Meals on the trail consisted of meat, potatoes, beans, biscuits, and cowboy coffee. Cowboy coffee was made by filling a pan full of water, adding a half dozen spoonfuls of coffee, and bringing it to a boil, then pouring the concoction into your cup. If you were lucky, the grounds would settle to the bottom.

The drives usually started from Millers, 20 miles southwest of Tonopah up the Smoky Valley. After we gathered the cattle, the drive would take a couple of days and one night. To hold the cows in place for the night, we would find a small open area, such as a salt marsh, and then everyone would take turns riding in a circle around the herd.

We decided on the general area where we would spend the night before we started the drive, so the cook could pull the chuck wagon and all our sleeping gear to that location ahead of time. When he arrived, the cowboys would throw their sleeping gear next to their saddles and sleep right on the ground around the campfire. We didn't have any fancy folding beds or blow-up mattresses, just a couple of blankets and our saddles for pillows.

Night riding meant constantly being alert to keep the herd from trying to break out and run back to where they had spent most of the winter. Some of the old seasoned cowboys would softly sing old cowboy songs to quiet the cows. This trick was also a way of keeping themselves awake after full days of riding.

The cook would set up his camp before we arrived with the herd. Carl had converted an old house trailer into a chuckwagon consisting of a kitchen and a long table on which to serve the meals family-style.

There was a memorable time when the cook showed up a little late at the chosen camp. I'm pretty sure he was drunk. I had hobbled my horse and was gathering dry pieces of sagebrush with which to build a fire.

As I made a bonfire out of the dried brush and cow patties, I looked up and saw the old truck. It was pulling the chuckwagon, bouncing down the dirt road to the rendezvous point. But there was a problem. When the truck's headlight beams hit the herd, they stampeded, heading straight back to their starting point of two days earlier.

I was scared to death. I was on foot during the stampede; my horse was tied up over the small hill, and I couldn't see him in the dark. I was standing all alone, cows thundering all around me, and tears running down my face. I think I was about 12 years old. I didn't want the other cowboys to see me, but I couldn't hide it. One of the cowhands helped me find my horse.

The slightly drunk cook helped me get the campfire going again. All the other cowboys got their sleeping gear and set up their places around the campfire, as there was no point in trying to find the cows in the dark. "No use crying over spilled milk" was the saying. The cook rustled up some grub, and we all sat around the fire, eating, laughing about the event, and drinking black coffee. We had a good night's sleep. In the morning we ate another good meal before heading back to round up the herd again and move them to the high country.

The work was long, hot, dusty, and dry. Most of the time my nose, ears, and mouth were filled with dust and sand.

We spent the hot days watching calves dart here and there and quickly galloping after them to reunite them with their mothers. The old bulls would get to fighting, and the herd would periodically try to break out. The skilled and seasoned cowboys, however, knew how to keep the herd moving and under control.

Each day offered a new lesson for me because there was always something happening that hadn't happened before. There were difficult times when I wasn't watching closely enough, and my horse would turn sharply to avoid sagebrush or a rock. Off him I would fly, headfirst into the rocky or sandy ground. I would try not to cry, but sometimes I did. The cowboys would all laugh, but I kept getting up, brushing off, and saddling up again. The old cowhands would comment, "Thatta boy! Cowboy up!"

After a couple of long days and nights, I was a tired buckaroo. I was ready for the trail drive to end so I could get back to a soft, clean bed after having eaten good grub in the warm and clean cookhouse.

Yet after the cattle drive, there still were plenty of jobs to be done. Some days we would brand the new calves. Other days, I would buck bales, tie sacks on the combine, or — everyone's favorite — shovel horse manure out of the barn.

There were a few more dramatic events on the ranch that would bring tears to my eyes. But I finally learned how to "cowboy up" and not cry. Instead, I got mad at the challenge and fought through the fear.

It prepared me for the frightening situations I would face in Vietnam, when my gunner and I would both be in tears over what looked like the end. Those tears, however, were not out of fear; they were more a release of tension that allowed me to reach inward for the learned skills and instincts to pull through the crisis. We would both laugh at ourselves for the tears in our eyes, but not say a word.

# CLOVERDALE

Cloverdale was my favorite of Carl's string of small ranches. Cloverdale was my favorite of Carl's string of small ranches. Though most of the old buildings were abandoned, the little ranch house, barn, corral were still usable, and the stream made it my secret getaway.

The time I spent at Cloverdale with Eddie Sherin and Don Ciarc was a wonderfully enjoyable experience. The three of us would haul the haying equipment onto the back of a trailer — the baler, a sickle, and a rake. Eddie would cut the grass with the sickle. He taught me how to sharpen the blades. I would pull the rake with the little old tractor that laid the hay in rows. Once the hay was cut and raked, Don would run the old baler and somehow keep it running. The three of us would stack bales the old-fashioned way. Don would drive the old flatbed truck, Eddie would toss the bales up to me on the back of the truck, and I would stack them as high as I could. We would then unload them in the barn. The wild grass hay was perfect for supplemental feed during the cold winters.

Cloverdale's location was right in the middle of the grazing lands allotted by the Bureau of Land Management.

Though there was an old ranch house on the property, we stayed outside. In the heat of the day, we wouldn't try to work but instead sat in the shade of the trees by the little creek that ran down from the mountains and through the meadows. Often the stream would dry up, but most of the time there was at least a little water to cool things off.

Don and Eddie would sleep in the ranch house, but I loved sleeping outside, usually on the back of the flatbed on an old mattress with a pillow and a light blanket. I was in Heaven. The stars were especially bright in this canyon.

We did all our cooking outside. Don was a master of the Dutch oven.

Don cooked the best cowboy stew in the world. Don would load the pot with every vegetable we could find in Ella's garden at the RO. He would cut up pieces of the deer we had just poached in the canyon, to be eaten during our stay. The best was his sourdough biscuits. Don even prepared excellent breakfasts using the metal grill on top of the outside fire. Eggs, ham, bacon, potatoes, you name it. I learned a lot from Don. He was from a fourth-generation mining family and had grown up in Manhattan, a quiet mining town about 10 miles south of the RO Ranch in Smokey Valley, Nevada. He learned all his skills in the old mining camps with his family. There are a few little shakes there, and, of course, the bar survived when the gold ran out.

Don was quite a character. He continued working with Carl when Carl was developing Kingston Canyon, and when Kingston was converted to a town, Don decided to run for mayor. He was very likable and intelligent and was considered a shoe-in. However, like Carl, Don had a vice: he was a heavy drinker. On the night before the election, when all the prospective voters were gathered in the only saloon in Kingston Village, Don got falling-down drunk, cussed out everyone, and told them he didn't need to take any of their advice; he would run his town the way he saw fit. The result: he got beaten by a write-in candidate!

While at Cloverdale, in the heat of the day I would work with my horse on roping or cutting calves in the corral. Though the mustangs were pretty wild, I learned to handle mine. Carl would not let me rope calves for practice at the RO because it was hard on them, but at Cloverdale, it was "out of sight, out of mind." Eddie and Don didn't care; they usually slept in the meadow during the heat of the day.

I loved my horse because he became a good cow horse. I had ridden for many years before I was confident that I would not get bucked off. It is said that "a 'good cowboy' does not get bucked off." I learned from Ed Fisher to climb in the middle of the horse and say to myself, "I am here to stay; I am like glue." Get rid of the fear and you become a good horseman. Once I gained this confidence, my horse and I would work many years together. I taught my horse to stay with the cow or keep on the calf, and he would jump sagebrush, sand hills, or rocks to get after them. There is no doubt in my mind that a horse knows when the rider is afraid. Once I recognized this, I felt that I would become a good cowboy.

Speaking of being considered a "real cowboy," I remember Carl telling me about the Michael Martin Murphey song, "Cowboy Logic," which included the following lyrics:

> An old cowboy and a young buckaroo were workin', ridin' fence
> The old hand was testin' the kid on his skill and common sense
> He said, "Son, if you seen three men in a pick-up truck
> Dressed alike from boot to hat
> Could you tell which one was the real cowboy just from where he sat? "

The kid scratched his head awhile and then he said
"Well, there ain't no way to know"
The old hand grinned and then he said
"Kid, you've still got a ways to go

The real cowboy's the one in the middle
He ain't there just by fate
'Cause first he don't have to drive
And then he don't have to mess with the gate."

    That was funny because, even when I was very young, I recall one occasion when Carl was taking a cattle buyer around the ranches. I quickly jumped in the middle of the seat of the pickup, with the purchaser on the side next to the door. Guess who had to get out and open and close all the gates?

    Carl usually gelded all of his ranch horses; they were sterile, but they kept their aggressive nature. Ed Fisher was a master at castration, making sure the horses would be able to work hard and live to maybe 18 or 19 years old. Carl himself had a thoroughbred stud, but I believed my mustang could outperform him because the thoroughbred always seemed too nervous or anxious. (No mares, because they made the geldings anxious; they would even break down a fence to get to a male horse.) Carl's horse was better in the corral, say, at roping and branding, but he didn't have endurance. My mustang didn't rein as well as Carl's horse, but get me in the flats or mountains and the difference in endurance was amazing. My mustang had tougher hooves and could handle rocks a lot better than Carl's horse.

    The three of us would spend about a week at Cloverdale, doing the haying and poaching a few deer. I would even sneak off and go upstream to catch a few rainbow trout for dinner. The canyon was not all that hot, especially in the evenings. Those days were a joy.

When I lived in Tonopah as a deputy district attorney and in private practice, I would often handle criminal cases in the Justice Court in Gabbs. A remaining mining town 100 miles north of Tonopah. I would take the old Pole Line Road, a dirt road in those days, going the back way to Gabbs. I would often swing by Cloverdale along the way and look around. Most of the old buildings were torn down, or have standing. But the corral and barn were kept up, as was the meadow for wild hay. I often thought about buying that ranch, but I remembered the words of my uncle: "A ranch owns you, you do not own it!"

No matter. Nothing ever took away my memories of Cloverdale, not even the hardships I faced in Vietnam and after. Most importantly, the memories consoled me when I found myself in the combat zone, hiding, waiting for rescue.

# LAST MEMORIES OF RANCH LIFE

During my final years of college, I spent a couple of summers cowboying, at least until Carl sold the RO, Miller's, Cloverdale, and Pevine ranches.

By this time, I considered myself to be an excellent horseman. How did I know that?

It was with assurance that I nestled myself firmly in the saddle and confidently turned my horse this way and that – forward and back, guiding the little calf to the right corral, my feet in the stirrups but with very little weight on them, holding steady, not a bit concerned about falling off the horse. No fear – and the horse knew it. That was when I knew I had the competence to be a horseman and work cattle – when I could gallop, turn my horse on a dime, catch the calf, and get it back to the herd. But that's not the best answer. The proof is in the pudding; true proficiency is when you can ride hard at a gallop, follow that calf anywhere, and stop and decide to get off the horse. I lift myself off the horse by placing my weight on the left stirrup and swinging my right leg over the saddle to step to the ground. However, instead of stepping to the ground as usual, to my surprise the saddle slides half way around the belly of the horse, Why is that? The cinch holding the saddle is loose and hanging down. Why didn't the saddle slip while I was chasing the calf or moving and turning at a gallop? Because I had kept my weight correctly centered in the saddle. I did not move my weight from one stirrup to the other; had I done that, the saddle would have slipped around, throwing me off. Excellent horsemen can ride with the saddle loosely cinched except when they get on and off. In my last days as a cowboy, I could do that!

I was lucky enough to be on one of the last ranches that actually herded cattle – not taking the herd from winter range to summer ranch by truck, but moving them by horse. What is herding? If you were to ask any individual on the street in the west what herding cattle is, most likely he or she would say, "Herding is the act of bringing different animals together into a group (herd), maintaining the group, and moving the group from place to place — or any combination of those." Ask a cowboy and he would say, "Pushing a bunch of dumb cows on a dusty, dirty, hot (or cold) day from one location to another for little pay."

As I worked more and more with moving cows, my earlier dreams of being a cowboy, with all its splendor, were quickly disappearing. The reality of riding behind moving cows in a cloud of trail dust offers not a whit of romance. The horse is sweating and smelly and kicking up dust; the mud or cow manure has an unyielding and disgusting odor, like sitting in an outhouse for too long. The cattle might be moving along pretty well, but then a couple of big bulls decide it is time to show who is the toughest, and they begin to fight. The herd starts to scatter, and all the cowboys gallop around, trying to keep the cows together. A young heifer decides to dart out of the herd and head back to where the drive started; one of the buckaroos heads her off and gets her back with the herd. Then a young calf decides it's his turn to head out, and again a cowpoke cuts it off. I try to break up the fighting bulls; one of them nicks my horse with a horn and the horse decides it's time to buck me off. I am seasoned and I expect that reaction, so after a little bucking, the horse ends up falling. I keep hold of the reins and pull up the horse, turn him around, swing back on, and give him a couple of kicks with the spurs; the horse settles down. That's a summary of the day-in and day-out job of herding cows. Not glamorous, but what a delightful memory and fun to talk about!

Daily life on a ranch included killing animals for food – chickens, sheep, steers, pigs, and even the occasional poached deer. This killing was a necessity, and it did not take long to accept it as normal. Later, as a warrior, I found that killing the enemy did not seem so wrong, either, especially when our attitude was to treat the enemy as animals or less than human. Once again, the last days of cowboying paved the way for my future survival.

My last days as a cowboy offer memories of the beauty of the desert. However, the desert can be just as deadly as it is magnificent. When the wind decides to blow, the highest thing in the flat land to slow it down is a two-foot sagebrush, so 50- to 60-mile-an-hour winds are not infrequent. Sudden dust storms were a common challenge. Sometimes a wind storm would last a few hours, other times just a short while. I recall a time riding along and gathering the cattle in the area assigned to me. I kept them bunched up and headed back to the corral or waterhole to load them into the cattle truck. Then, I noticed dust four or five miles away. Before I knew it, the wind storm hit me, my horse, and the cows I had gathered. The dust was so thick I couldn't see the cows that were right in front of me. My horse started jumping and bucking; I kept trying to get control. I grabbed the bandana from around my neck and pulled it through the bridle to protect my horse's eyes from the sand. However, because I had only one bandana, plenty of sand got into my eyes, nose, and ears. I tried to find a little hill or gully to pull my horse into and away from the intense blinding winds. The few head of cattle I had gathered took off, trying to find whatever shelter they could. On several occasions, older cowboys had to come over to my area to see if I was all right. They'd help me with my horse, and when the wind stopped, they'd help me round up the cows I had gathered earlier.

There was no reprieve in the winter, either. The cold winter days usually had white-out blowing snow, which did essentially the same thing, except instead of dust, dirt, and sand in my nose, eyes, and ears, the freezing snow would cake up on my face and hands, eventually covering my entire body. Arduous as these experiences were, talking about it still brings joy to my life!

If you have never been in the open desert and felt the "hush," that void of sound that seems so silent you're sure you can hear the lizard running, the rabbit hopping, or the snake crawling, you've missed one of life's pleasures! The desert is amazing; every once in a while, usually when the cowboys were riding side by side heading out in the early morning, they would split up to cover their assigned areas alone and hear the "desert hush!" In *The Quiet American*, Graham Greene wrote, "So it always is: when you escape to a desert the silence shouts in your ear." The silence is deafening. A strange word to use, but how else is one to explain this uncanny silence — the horse's hooves softly plodding along on the desert sand; the swishing of his tail as he swats at flies; a slight snapping of the reins on the side of the saddle; the jingling of the spurs; maybe a gentle wind. However, the calmness as the cowboy rides alone is the real secret – the beauty of being with all of nature's glory. If every day had been like that, we would still have an abundance of cowboys and cattle ranches. But in central Nevada, the days are usually windy. Often, thunderstorms frighten the cattle and make them scatter, with two or three days' work required to gather them all over again. The dust devils twist and blow the tumbleweeds hither and thither, often jabbing one's horse with their sharp barbs, making him buck. In spite of all the dust and wind, those few eerie silent mornings bring me back to the desert year after year, even if only in my memories.

Then there were the cowboy jokes:

> A horse buyer goes to a little ranch to buy a horse. He spots a beautiful horse in the field and asks, "How much for the horse?"
> The owner says that the horse "don't look good!"
> The buyer says, "What are you trying to do, jack up the price? That is a wonderful horse. I want to buy it."
> "Ok," says the owner, "but it don't look good." The owner takes $100 and loads the horse.
> The next day the new owner mounts the magnificent horse and it runs right into a fence. The buyer takes the horse back, telling the seller, "This horse is as blind as a bat!"
> Hearing this, the seller responds, "I told you it don't look good!"

An old cowboy is at the dentist:

"What do you think, doc?"
"Well, you have a couple of teeth that are broken or so abscessed they are going to have to be pulled."
"Ok, go ahead and pull them out."
"Open up and let's put a little Novocain to kill the pain."
"No, that is all right, I have only felt pain twice in my life."
First tooth out, blood spurts everywhere. The dentist says, "You cannot tell me that did not hurt!"
"Oh, it smarted a little, but I have really felt pain only twice in my life."
Out comes the second tooth. Again, blood spurts. The dentist shakes his head, feeling sorry for the cowboy, saying, "Ok, if that was not painful, what pain did you feel twice in your life?"
"Well," says the cowboy, "I was riding in the mountains one summer and decided to get off my horse and relieve myself. I pulled my pants down and squatted down and set right in the middle of a bear trap. That was the first."
"Then, what was the second?" asked the dentist.
"When I hit the end of the chain!"

The three lies a cowboy tells:

I won this belt buckle at the rodeo! All the payments on my pickup are paid up! I was just helping the sheep over the fence!

Why is the bottle of Jack Daniels square?
So it won't roll around on the floorboard of your pick-em-up-truck!

# WARRIOR TIMES

# START YOUR AIRCRAFT

My gunner and I slowly walked to our aircraft after the morning briefing. We didn't talk much — we just quietly walked and thought about the mission. That morning's briefing informed us about enemy movement in the area where we would be scouting; we all knew we would encounter a lot of enemy fire. That was part of our job — to seek out and destroy the enemy. We, pilots and gunners alike, all found ways to cope with this reality of war.

The early morning, as usual, was damp, and humid, the air filled with the odor of rotten vegetation and musky smoke — probably from areas burning after a bomb strike, or farmers burning weeds in the rice paddies. The aircraft sat alone, reminding me of the many war machines I had read about in my school days: contraptions such as chariots, war wagons, or a World War I massive tank. It brought to mind a line by one of my favorite poets, Jody Parker. "War machines battle on this forgotten place, lost between the anchors of time."

My light observation helicopter was the Oh6, or, as it was called "the Loach." (It received this name because it looked a bit like a fish tadpole.) My helicopter had a machine mini-gun secured at one side. This killing device was capable of firing 2000 rounds a minute. (Unlike the six-barrel Gatling guns in the old war movies that turned over with hand cranks, it had an electric motor activated by a trigger.) Sticking out of the open back door of the other side was my gunner's M60, a 30-caliber machine gun hanging from a bungee cord over the right back seat, occupied by the gunner. In the back with the gunner were several cases of concussion and white phosphorus grenades, as well as smoke grenades of all colors. And don't forget those homemade bombs, all strapped to the deck, easily accessible.

The gunner and I were dressed in our fireproof flight gear with bullet-proof vests that had been proven to stop a 30-caliber bullet. We carried our helmets under our arms. I was packing my 38-caliber sidearm in a shoulder holster under my left arm. My gunner was carrying the aforementioned M60 machine gun, which would hook to the bungee cord at the entrance to his back seat. That way, he could easily reach out to his side and spray enemy positions.

Breaking the Geneva Convention rules, I also packed an enemy weapon — a Czechoslovakian automatic pistol with a 30-round clip, in a holster strapped to my right side. I had obtained this enemy weapon from a Marine who had taken it off an enemy "sapper" whom the Marine had killed after the sapper had tried to crawl under barbed wire to set a bomb in our compound. ("Sapper" is a term used to describe an enemy-trained infiltrator; I never found out how those little sneaks got the name.) The Marine gave me the pistol as thanks for letting him fly with me on a combat mission (albeit one that almost got us killed).

The stillness of the flight-line was uncanny. All the pilots and gunners were walking to their aircraft, keeping their thoughts and words to themselves, preparing for the day's hunter/killer team mission.

These otherwise hidden feelings were often disguised as jokes, or by laughter over the stupid things we had all done during the previous evening's drunken party. These feelings influenced the way we dreamed up outrageous descriptions of a girl's beauty: "I would crawl through a minefield, climb over barbed wire fences, fight off alligators — just to smell the tire track of the garbage truck that carried her tampon away!" We would also conjure up sayings when our tour was getting close to ending. "I'm so short, I need a ladder to get on the first step of the entrance to my hooch."

Nevertheless, the nervous tension did not interfere with the task at hand. After carefully examining my aircraft using the pre-flight checklist, I put my leg on the front floorboard and reached up for the handle to pull myself into my war machine.

We arrived at the point where my gunner and I were sitting in our aircraft, awaiting the radio command to start the engine. I pulled on my helmet and tightened the chinstrap. I adjusted the microphone attached to the helmet so that it was not too far or too close to my lips. With the help of the gunner, I buckled my shoulder harness and fastened the seatbelt. I made sure the pedals operating the tail rotor were the right length for my short legs.

I followed each of these precise steps to dispel my inner nervousness and fear of what might occur once we found the enemy. Later, soon after taking off, I would test-fired my mini-gun. I focused in front where the rounds would land. Using a black marker, I affixed a little "X" on my fiberglass front to see how far in front of the helicopter the bullets would hit. This makeshift marking acted as a gun-sight and allowed me to shoot, aim, and hit where I wanted as I guided the aircraft to the enemy's position.

All of a sudden, the silence was broken by the radio. The command rang in my earphones: "Start your aircraft." An instant later came the nerve-shattering, thunderous, high-pitched noise of five jet turbo-engines igniting, along with the eardrum-breaking whooping uproar as the whirling rotor blades joined in. The smoke from the exhaust replaced the pungent smoke from the bombing or burning weeds. Like a choreographed group of dancers, the helicopters slowly rose in unison to a hover. The nose of each aircraft lowered simultaneously, then pulled up and majestically rose into the sky. The gunships and command ship would climb over 1500 feet, out of the range of small guns. However, we scouts remained about 10 to fifteen feet above the ground, always surveying the terrain for any evidence of enemy movement.

Once we were far enough from the base, we would find an open field and test the mini-gun and M60. When test-firing our guns, we sang Dean Martin's "Everybody Loves Somebody":

> "Everybody loves somebody sometimes"... *Ratatat...ratatat...*" Everybody falls in love somehow"... *Ratatat...ratatatat...* "Something in your kiss just told me my sometime is now...*Ratatat...ratatat...*"Everybody finds somebody someplace...*Ratatat...ratatat...* "There's no telling where love may appear/Something in my heart keeps saying my someplace is here"...*Ratatat...ratatat...*

Each time we squeezed the trigger, we sang the same words. We used this song to make light of a distressingly grim task. Nonetheless, kill or be killed was the rule!

As the days, weeks, and months passed, I noticed that I was changing dramatically. I began to wonder how long it would be before the pressure got to me. Would I break? When would I realize that the trauma had changed me forever, and how would it affect my life? How many days would I spend thinking, 'This day may be my last'? War was draining me of my humanity. One thing was for sure: I vowed to do whatever it took not to die in this stinking country.

I would last. I would survive — but not without a terrible blow to my spirit and a dark lack of love for humankind. Amid the horrors of war, I believe that to some degree, the dangers of being a cowboy helped me cope a little better than some of my fellow soldiers did. I had faced risks daily on the ranch, so I was prepared. Oh, and, of course, there was always the cheap booze at the makeshift officers' club in the compound!

# PREDESTINED

I was predestined to fly. When I was only six or seven years old, there was no stopping me from climbing to the top of the windmill or the water tower. I wanted to get as high as I could and see as far as I could. My downfall, however, was that every time I climbed high, my loving dog and constant companion, Pumpkin, would bark and then out would come my grandmother. The switch from the willow let me know such acts would not be tolerated!

At 16, with financial assistance from my uncle, I took flying lessons at the Tonopah Airport, 40 miles from Coaldale and 200 miles from Las Vegas. I became a pilot a year later. I learned in a tail-dragging Super Cub PA-18. After I soloed and needed practice, I got as much flying in as possible. One day was unusual; the wind started blowing hard and I needed to land. However, when I came into land and lowered the tail as I slowed down, the plane lifted again. The plane was so light and the wind so strong that when I cut the power and lifted the nose of the plane to land, it kept flying. The wind over the wing, or the airfoil, kept the aircraft in the air when the nose pointed up as the tail was lowered. I called the tower and asked if the guys could go out and hold me down. What a scene – it was just like hovering in a helicopter in front of the FAA building in Tonopah. If I tried to lower my tail, the aircraft would simply lift up again, so the guys ran out and grabbed my plane on each side by the wheels. I cut my engine, and they pulled the plane to the ground. What a laugh!

I learned a few things about flying the hard way. One lesson was that taxiing a tail dragger too fast will "ground loop" it. This phrase describes what the aircraft does – spins around like a top. It's even possible to flip the aircraft over. I managed to ground loop the Super Cub once, and that was enough!

When I was in college, I transitioned to my uncle's Cessna Turbo 210: the workhorse of the sky. I grew proficient in flying investors to Kingston Canyon, my uncle's land development in Smoky Valley. Unbeknownst to me at the time, this land development would be where I ended up after active duty in the Army.

A memorable aerial trip occurred about the time I started college. My uncle sold the Super Cub to a priest in Canada, and it was up to me to fly it from Reno to Penticton, 1,000 miles. If he put pontoons or skis on it, the Super Cub would be a perfect plane for the priest to use in getting to all the little villages in Canada.

My solo 10-hour flight was difficult. I didn't have many hours flying or navigating. However, I kept focused on landmarks all the way and delivered the plane safely.

The story didn't have a happy ending, though. A few months after I flew the plane to the priest, I heard that as the priest was traveling around Canada, the kids in the villages became so excited to see him that they would run out to greet him as soon as he landed. Unfortunately, they did not know to stay clear of the propellers, and on one trip, before the priest could get the engine shut down, a little girl walked right into the propeller and was killed instantly. The priest could not bring himself to fly again for some time.

As I grew, in addition to wanting to climb on everything, I loved to drive very fast. I also longed to be flying. These interests supported my belief that I was predestined to be an Army Man. This view was reinforced when I did well at my college preparatory high school, San Rafael Military Academy, north of San Francisco. That school gave me the opportunity to play football, run track, and compete in tennis, things I could not have done living 40 miles from Tonopah

How clearly I recall the day I left the ranch for high school. Another cowboy and I had ridden out very early to mend fences. I was tightening the barbed wire while the other cowboy hammered the nail into the post when I noticed an old pickup truck bouncing across the field. There was no road; that is why we rode out with our horses. Regardless, here came the truck, driven by Uncle Carl. When he pulled up next to us, besides spooking the horses, he said, "It's time to go. You have to get ready to fly to San Francisco and enroll in school. I need to drive you to Tonopah, where your mother is waiting for you. She has packed your things, and I have loaded your suitcase with the items you brought here. The flight was changed, and you have to leave early to drive to Reno, and fly to San Francisco."

All I could think about was leaving my horse, an animal that had been my soulmate and companion for years. Though I was nearly 15 years old, I was almost in tears. I asked the cowboy who was with me to please take care of my horse and gear, and I would see him on my first vacation and bring him a bottle of whiskey. He laughed and said everything would be okay. To this day, I think that leaving my horse was just as sad as leaving my dog, Pumpkin. Remembering my first few months alone at night without my dog at the foot of my bed, made me so lonely, I even cried.

\  pumpkin

There I was, this rough-and-ready cowboy, far from the ranch I loved and from my horse and dog — very homesick! Still, I would cowboy up and soon fit right in. I would make lifelong friends and enjoy four great years.

I arrived at school a couple of weeks early so that I could go out for the freshman football team. After my mother dropped me off and I got settled in my room, the adventure started. I did not have a great beginning. I understood that I would be wearing a cadet uniform, but after arriving, I learned we would not get our uniforms for a couple of weeks, when school started. We were allowed to wear civilian clothes during football practice. However, there was a requirement that short-sleeve shirts and slacks were the only garments allowed in the mess hall. All I had were my long-sleeve western shirts and Levis. When I was not allowed in for lunch, I almost cried. Luckily, the dean was walking by and was close enough to see and hear what was going on. He introduced himself and asked me if he could take me to Sears and help me get a couple of pairs of slacks and some short-sleeve dress shirts. I told him I would be grateful. So off we went.

After that day, I had an ideal relationship with the dean. In fact, when I was working as a counselor at school the last summer before I graduated, I was assigned 12 boys to my dorm for summer camp. Our dorm passed all the courses with the highest grades and received the highest scores on our daily inspections, so we won a three-day trip to Yosemite National Forest, paid for by the dean. The dean and I drove the vans with our kids, pulling trailers with our camping gear.

After arriving, we watched the dean try to back one of the trailers into the parking space; he was having a heck of a time. He got out of the van, mad as a hornet, then came to me and said that if I could back up hay wagons, I should be able to back up anything. I agreed and backed the trailer in like a pro. Everyone cheered me and laughed at the dean.

We all slept in tents while the dean rented a beautiful log cabin down the road. After arriving, I gave my kids an order to set up camp in ship shape. If the camp wasn't perfect when I came back in an hour, there was going to be trouble. I walked down to the dean's cabin, where I knocked on the door and heard a rustling around. When the dean opened the door, I saw a woman in the back of the room. None of us said a word, but after that day, until graduation, whenever I asked a favor of the dean, such as leaving early to catch a plane for vacation, he granted it. I even had a private car on campus the month before graduation.

Getting this car was due to a bit of luck. Many of us seniors snuck cars to school and parked them across the street in a synagogue's parking lot. One day when I was running up the alley across from the parking lot holding our cars, heading to PE class, I saw the assistant dean taking down the license plates of the cars. Apparently, the synagogue attendees had made complaints about the cars on their property. I skipped PE and returned to my room, changed back into my uniform, and headed to the dean's office. I confessed that I had a car in the synagogue parking lot, I failed to ask permission to keep it in the school parking lot as another student had done. The dean said, "Okay, but park it on the school grounds and drive only on weekends." I agreed and moved the car. Once the assistant dean found out who owned the other vehicles parked next to the school, they were called before the dean and suspended for two days. I never told them of my trick with the dean, when I was lucky enough to see the assistant dean writing down the license plates on those cars in the parking lot.

Though the young boys from my dorm had won the camping trip, the experience wasn't entirely fun. I constantly warned the kids not to eat in their tents. One little boy didn't listen. On the second day of our camping trip, at about 2:00 in the morning, an earth-shattering scream came from his sleeping area. Sure enough, he was eating, and a bear had entered the camp, smelling the food. When the boy sat up, the bear struck him on the side of the head with a massive paw. The claws ripped three large cuts in the kid's head, cuts that needed stitches. We had to rush him to the closest emergency room. Within a couple of hours, his parents had driven up from San Francisco to take him home. I never saw him again.

After the incident, the other boys and I hiked and stayed at a couple of other campsites high in the majestic Yosemite Park. We had fun hiking and enjoying the beautiful mountains and sights, but there wasn't much to laugh about.

I had great success at San Rafael Military Academy. I was the commander of the drill team when I was a junior. We performed in the Veteran's Day parade in San Francisco and won first place for a high school military group. I went from a C- average my freshman year to the Honor Roll my senior year. My grade point average and a decent score on the college entrance exam got me accepted at the University of Nevada.

As was my way, a slow beginner, I had study issues at first. Can you imagine going from a military academy to the party life at the University of Nevada? Nevertheless, I kept my grades high enough to graduate. After completing the first two years of mandatory ROTC, I was accepted into Advanced ROTC and would receive a commission in the United States Army upon graduation. I again excelled in ROTC, being promoted my senior year to Cadet Lieutenant

Colonel, commander of the counter-guerrilla team. This unit would ambush the regular troops in training exercises. I enjoyed the military structure and learned it well. It seemed that an Army career was for me.

After graduation, I was ordered to attend Fort Sill Oklahoma for the officer's Field Artillery basic training course. In the 1970s, the only way to get into army aviation was to get into a combat branch.

However, about six months before I graduated and was set to go on active duty in the Army, I met and fell in love with a beautiful girl named Linda. I saw her several times at the University and one day she, and a girlfriend came into the Pizza Oven when I was tending bar. She was a knock-out, and so I made the moves. She was not taking the moves, but came in a few more times and finally agreed to a date. I took her to the nicest place in town, almost broke me, but that did it, and the dating was on. I even bought her a puppy.

However, before I left for officer basic training, I knew that becoming a pilot meant I would most likely go to Vietnam. I told Linda we should wait to get married until I get back from Vietnam and that she should stay in Reno. She reluctantly agreed, so off I went to Fort Sill. However, that plan didn't last long; after a week at Fort Sill, calling Linda every night, one evening I said, "What the hell, it will be a least a year before Vietnam, so let's get married and enjoy the year."

I drove back to Reno, got married in the Reno Wedding Chapel, marring Linda Jean Parr on August 28, 1970;

and went back to Oklahoma in a round trip that took four grueling days. The marriage turned out great. I would not die in Vietnam; I would make it through law school, and at the time I am writing this book, Linda and I are sneaking up on our 46${}^{th}$ year of marriage! One year at a time.

After I had completed the six-month artillery officer basic course at Fort Sill, my application to become an army aviator was accepted. But there was still that feared first medical examination. Vision must be 20/20, no colorblindness, good depth perception, proper weight, and overall good health. The test was performed and I passed, so then I was off to Mineral Wells, Texas, the first primary helicopter training school, near Dallas/Fort Worth. The desert countryside was almost identical to Coaldale Junction's, so I felt at home. We also found Carmen's bar, just like Coaldale's. We would become shuffleboard champs in our off time. We liked Carmen's better than the stuffy officer's club.

Flight school began with my going into the classroom and learning about the principles of the helicopter or rotorcraft. What is a cockpit, cabin, skid, tail boom, tail rotor, main rotor, rotor blade, stabilizer bar, swashplate, mast, cowl, drive shaft, 45-degree gearbox, 90-degree gearbox, cross tube, fuselage, collective, cyclic, pedal? A new world, indeed. Though I had acquired several hundred hours in fixed-wing planes, I soon realized that flying a helicopter was much different. I could not fly any better than those who had never flown.

The first and hardest task was learning to hover. I had to lift the craft a couple of feet off the ground and keep it there.

The physical training began with the instructor teaching us how to do a thorough pre-flight check. I was then shown how to start the engine. The instructor lifted the craft to a hover, showing me how each of the controls worked. My instructor stressed that I must use the lightest touch on all the controls. Each control was accomplished by the trainer, then by the student, repeatedly. First, with my feet, I would press the anti-torque pedals that controlled the tail rotor; this kept me from spinning around because of the torque of the main rotor blade. Next, the instructor gave me control of the cyclic, the stick-like device between my legs. Then he had me lift and lower the aircraft with the collective, the tubular bar on the left side of the seat. The collective is also the location of the power control or throttle for increasing the speed of the rotor. With my right hand on the cyclic, my left hand on the collective, and my feet on the pedals, I tried to maintain control of the craft. Up and down I went, sometimes in a circle, working as hard as I could to get the hang of hovering. Suddenly, the helicopter would oscillate like crazy, and I would hear the instructor say, "I have the controls." The instructor took control of the aircraft. Again, and again, he instructed me by saying that I had to be very light on the controls: "You fly with pressures, not movements." There is a short time lag between making a control movement and the helicopter's reaction. Many hours are needed to master the art of hovering, but my classmates and I stayed on track and passed each phase of the training.

Then came the scary part — learning autorotation. There are four steps in the autorotation process: entry, glide, flare, and collective pull to a touchdown or power recovery. The instructor cut the power and bottomed the collective (which flattened the main rotor blade), and the helicopter dropped like a rock. Just before it seemed the thing would crash, the instructor pulled up on the collective, the main rotor grabbed the air, the descent stopped, and the aircraft landed softly on the ground. But that was when the instructor did it. It took many hard landings for me to learn how to do it myself.

Then there was my first solo flight. The instructor got out of the helicopter and said, "Give me a couple of touches and goes." I twisted the power control to full power, then, nervously lifted the craft to a hover, keeping it about two feet off the ground and in one place as much as possible. I used every muscle in my body to keep the aircraft from bouncing off. Then I slowly pulled up on the collective, nudged the nose slightly forward, and up and forward I went. I flew down the runway, climbed to about 500 feet, circled, and returned at a hover to where I had started. I repeated the move three or four times. After I had completed the solo flight, we put the aircraft away and the instructor at de-briefing did the traditional cutting of the tail of my shirt. On the patch he wrote my name, his name, and the date of the solo flight. I kept that piece for years; I may still have it somewhere. All that was left was to get out each day and build up solo hours before advancing to the next stage.

Having completed the core course, I was off to Fort Rucker, Alabama, the primary Army aviation school, and getting to know the "Huey," the primary transport helicopter used to move ground troops. I would go through the same process — hover and autorotate — over and over again, just in another aircraft. This time, however, two students and the instructor were on the plane. Each student would take turns learning to fly the aircraft. We would solo fly together, working hard not to kill each other. Our training included combat flying, night flying, and formation flying.

In the southern United States in 1970, prejudice was still alive, I was pleased to have one of the first black pilots as my "stick buddy." I have to give the Army credit for knowing that a cowboy from Coaldale didn't have a racist bone in his body. I just wanted both of us to avoid killing each other while we were learning. By sharing our fears, we developed an incredible bond. Our wives were just as close, knowing what we were going through each day.

The scariest event was when my stick buddy and I did our first solo night practice mission. We had to take off and land at numerous checkpoints. If we missed one, we would fail. Though both of us were very nervous, we passed the course. However, that night was not so good because learning to fly combat missions was miserable. My entire class, maybe 20 aircraft, was doing the same exercise that first night. Each of us had to complete checking in and landing at each checkpoint. That evening, in two separate locations, two of our fellow student pilots must have gotten vertigo or fixated without realizing it, for they flew their aircraft directly into the ground, killing everyone on board.

Experiencing the death of comrades first hand brought home to me the dangers of flying in combat. It also taught us a lesson in dealing with the passing of a classmate and understanding that each comrade's wife or girlfriend had lost a partner, or his children a father.

After the incident, the base commander took the whole class into the main hangar and reminded us that flying is dangerous and that flying in combat is even more so. However, we had to persevere and do our duty. The words did not help, and the sadness did not go away quickly. From the first loss to the many other losses I have experienced, it never got easier.

Flight school had well-trained instructors. All these pilots had flown in Vietnam and survived. They demanded perfection. Whenever a task was assigned, the instructor would show us once how it was done and then it was up to the student pilot to remember and do it right. When I returned from Vietnam and became an instructor pilot, I remembered and applied many of the techniques my first flight instructors had taught me. I then passed those techniques on to my students.

On one hilarious day, we were practicing our solo flying at Fort Walters, in the core course. Each student was given routes and checkpoints to follow. Our class leader was a captain. Like the rest of us, he was on his solo cross-country flight. He apparently had some problems. As he told us:

> I was lost and couldn't find checkpoints or even figure out which way to go when I spotted a gas station alongside the road. I knew I was running short on gas, so I landed next to the station and bought five gallons of gas that the owner helped put in the tank with a funnel. He gave me a road map and showed me the way back to base. I really got hell from maintenance for using regular and not aviation gas. I got a reprimand and was relieved of being a class leader, but I wasn't kicked out of flight school, probably because I did a year in Vietnam as a ground pounder.

As I progressed through flight school, I recognized that those things I had learned on the ranch would help me cope with the rigors of training. For example, I had been trained to be careful when working around the baler, or the combine; a hand put in the wrong place amid all the moving parts could cost me that hand. Likewise, not paying attention to the moving rotor blade or tail rotor could cost me my life. My learning to stay steady on a horse that was half broken prepared me to maintain complete control of the aircraft at all times. Respecting the machine and relying on my training was the same, whether it applied to flying or cowboying – stay focused and pay attention or you could lose your life.

Graduation from flight school arrived. My wife and I were so excited about my getting my wings! Sadly, the day before graduation, we heard that Linda's dad had died. She had to go home to be with her family and attend the funeral, so she missed my graduation. However, after graduation, I took a two-week course at Fort Knox, Kentucky, learning to fly the Loach OH-6 helicopter. I also learned about the use of the mini-gun. The base was close enough for me to drive to Sikeston, where Linda's family lived and where she was staying, so I could see my wife on the weekends. It was a happy and sad time, but we made the most of it. My brother-in-law, Eddie Ray, met me with a bottle of Jack Daniels when I arrived early in the morning. We spent the rest of the day drinking and meeting his relatives, who accounted for half the town. Though a tough riverboat captain, he would die just a few years later at the age of 46. To the end, he was one of my real friends. Linda was devastated to lose her dad and then a few years later her oldest brother. Linda's twin brother was in the Navy and returned from Vietnam, but was diagnosed with PTSD and would die by suicide at the young age of 36.

After the two-week training, Linda and I loaded up our car and headed home to Reno. We bought a condominium at Smithridge, where she would live while I was in Vietnam. This unit would be a good investment. When I started law school we sold the condo and was able to use the extra money to lived.

# HELLO VIETNAM

All my training was complete. There was a great condo for Linda in Reno and orders to report to Travis Air Force Base to be transported to Vietnam in my pocket. The trip was a disaster from the start. My wife and I loaded our car with my uniforms and gear, then drove the 200 miles from Reno to Travis. The uncomfortable moment of getting out of the car and seeing my wife drive away — not knowing if that would be the last time I saw her — is still fresh in my memory 40 years later.

But, as is always the case in the military, Murphy's Law triumphed! After two hours of waiting to depart, we were told that the aircraft had mechanical problems and the flight would not leave until the following afternoon. So I took a cab back to Reno, stopping at a liquor store for a six-pack on the way. I showed up at the condo, and when Linda answered the door, she nearly had a heart attack.

We turned up the stereo, finished off the beer I brought, then broke out the wine. We called the Pizza Oven and had a large pizza delivered. We spent the evening singing and dancing. We made the second sad trip back to Travis Base the next day.

By then the transport plane had been repaired, and we headed to Vietnam, with a fuel stop in Thailand. There were 50 or so enlisted men and 20 officers on the 20-plus-hour trip. We were able to stretch our legs while refueling and grabbed as many shots at the bar as we could before the final leg to Saigon.

Again, Murphy's Law struck! No one had bothered to contact headquarters in Vietnam regarding the flight change. There were no buses or personnel to meet us. A couple of the men were on their second tour but had never landed in Saigon before. All they knew was that buses were supposed to take us to Camp Alpha. That was where everyone would get an orientation and unit assignment.

There I was, looking around, imagining that each Vietnamese person I saw was ready to shoot me. Some of the other newbies felt the same way. Finally, the senior officers found out where the buses usually picked up the arriving soldiers. We exchanged our dollars for Vietnamese currency, called Dong. Then we piled into the buses and headed to Camp Alpha.

At Camp Alpha, everyone was assigned to a barracks, given sheets and blankets, and shown where the mess hall was. We were told to check with headquarters every day until command had decided where to assign us.

I knew that the Air Force base had an ungraded officer's club and air conditioned apartments for their officer across the bases, so with one of my new friends, Lieutenant Bill Hartman, I caught a ride to the nearest Air Force facility. We arrived at the officers' club and the drinking started. Bill and I met a couple of Air Force pilots who said they were being deployed up north for a couple of weeks and that we were welcome to use their air-conditioned room with two bunks and a private bath. We got our gear from Camp Alpha and settled in at the Air Force base.

So here I found myself, finally in Vietnam, an area of Northeast Asia where war had been ongoing, starting with the French in the 1950s. The Americans had begun as advisors in the early 1960s, but ended up sending several hundred thousand troops to prevent the North Vietnamese communists from invading the South. I did not arrive until late 1971 and I left in 1972. America pulled out in about 1973-74. Within months, the South fell to the North.

Thus our tours of duty in the combat zone started. However, as the days went by and daily check-ins never changed from "come back tomorrow and we will know more," we got worried. Cash was running low.

I finally went to the commander's office. I told the commander we had been just sitting around for days, not getting an assignment to any unit. Nor did we have any way to get our pay. The commander was outraged to hear this and immediately took action. The officers were asked where they would like to be assigned. Because I had been given additional training to transition into the scout helicopter "Loach," I was sure I would be assigned to an Air Cavalry Unit flying my OH6 observation helicopter.

With lots of firepower,

Attached to the left side was an M134 mini-gun (a 7.62-by-51mm NATO six-barrel machine gun) attached to the left side.

My gunner in the back seat wielded his 30-calibre M60:

So, goodbye to the officers' club, air-conditioning, bathroom, and drinks. Hello, F Troop 8th US Air Cavalry.

The members of F Troop 8th Calvary were called the Blue Ghosts. Each of us received a "call sign" that we would use when talking on the radio. My call sign was BLUE GHOST 17.

My cavalry hat hangs on my wall today.

Our unit was assigned to the hottest combat area in North Vietnam — the main base Da Nang, with a combat outpost in the province of Quang Tri City. This province was the northernmost village still controlled by the South Vietnamese government… at least when I first arrived.

I had no idea what was going to happen to me when I got into combat; I saw every Vietnamese person as an enemy. I checked in with the company executive officer (or XO) and was given my 38-revolver sidearm and ammo. I was then assigned to the officers' barracks.

Home                                    Raley's

I would find some snacks in the makeshift company store.

As a scout, I would be in a hunter-killer team. What in the hell is a hunter-killer Air Cav unit? It combines the tasks of finding targets and attacking them. The technique involved sending a Loach or two on a low-level mission to follow trails or a specified area where the enemy may have been spotted by an Air Force reconnaissance plane. The scout then attempts to flush out the enemy positions, flying three to four feet from the ground, sometimes dropping a homemade bomb in the free-fire area. Free-fire was an area, authorized by the command, where we could shoot at anything that moved. We could also use our bombs there.

The homemade bomb consisted of a white phosphorus grenade

C-4 explosive charge and a quart can of hydraulic fluid.

The C-4 was wrapped around the hydraulic fluid can and the grenade was taped to the top. Pull the pin and throw it out. The bombs were brutal. The white phosphorus could not be put out with water; it would only keep burning until finished. The only way to stop the burning was to take a knife and cut the piece out of one's body. If the enemy was in the area where we dropped our bomb, the survivors would shoot at us. When that happened, we would get out of there as fast as possible.

We would then drop the smoke grenade to mark the enemy position as close as possible as we left, calling out "taking fire" so that the gunships flying above us could direct their machine gun fire or lay down rockets in that area. The gunship was

 called a Cobra.

The combat helicopter was equipped with as many as four missiles on each small wing on the left and right of the fuselage. It also had a machine gun on the bottom front. A pilot sat in the front seat and a gunner in the back. It is truly a "killing machine."

I recall a story told by one of the officers who was giving us a briefing before a mission. This officer said that he had interviewed an enemy colonel, who apparently staggered into a base camp all shot up and dirty, with his uniform torn. The colonel kept mumbling over and over, "If I told them once, I have told them a hundred times; don't shoot at that type of helicopter." There is no doubt in my mind that it was the Cobra to which this battered soldier referred.

Also flying above us was the Huey. Aboard was the duty officer or company commander Blue Ghost 16, an interpreter and the local village leader.

 Command Huey

The command ship ensured that the hunter-killer team was in the right area, and was authorized to fire on the targets or return enemy fire.

Less than three weeks after being assigned to Da Nang, and flying out of Quang Tri province, all I had done was "taxi" duty: flying generals or senior officers to their meetings. However, before I knew it, our outpost in Quang Tri had been overrun by North Vietnamese troops. They captured the first provincial capital during the Offense of 1972. We lost several aircraft during the attack, as well as several lives.

F Troop 8th Cav. managed to get all troops and equipment back to the main base at Da Nang. We continued to run combat missions from there, and I was suddenly assigned to combat missions to look for the enemy. Two of my fellow scouts and their gunners died in the offensive. In less than four months in the country, I ended up being the most senior officer in the Loach platoon. I was to take over as a platoon leader.

Initially, the South Vietnamese defenders were almost overwhelmed, particularly in the northernmost provinces, where they abandoned their positions in Quang Tri. However, it took weeks of bitter fighting, with the South Vietnamese soldiers suffering heavy casualties before they managed to hold their own with the aid of U.S. advisers and American air power.

F troop, however, never re-deployed to Quang Tri. The tallest building still standing by the time the troop left was about five feet high. The roads from Quang Tri to Da Nang were cluttered with the burning and damaged carts and vehicles of civilians who were trying to flee the invading Northern Vietnamese.

We were used to fighting guys in black pajamas, not soldiers fully equipped and heavily armed with AK-47s, rocket launchers, and tanks and personnel carriers. They were truly an invading army.

As luck would have it, F Troop had been assigned a single unique helicopter unit: a crew of two pilots and a chief gunner equipped with a new type of missile wire designed for destroying tanks.

I led the way, as usual, heading to the north in a hunt for tanks, the copter right behind me. Soon enough, I spotted a couple of tanks in the open. I marked the area with smoke and got out of there. For the first time after having sat around for two months doing nothing, this crew would get to show its stuff. How would they blow up a tank? First, they had to keep the aircraft steady, even when taking fire, then aim and shoot their wire-guided rockets at the tank. They disabled the two tanks and got back unharmed. This bravery by American forces assisted the Southern Vietnamese Marines in retaking Quang Tri, though there was not much to retake. The wire-guided rocket crew never encountered any other tanks on the tour.

The real problem with flying in far North Vietnam's theater of operations was that it was all jungle. If my aircraft were shot down, there would be no place to land. Crashing into the trees would surely mean death.

It wasn't until I was in Vietnam, under heavy fire while on a "scout" — a hunter/killer mission – that I would reap the benefits of what I had learned as a young cowboy.

After losing several pilots and crew in the Quan Tri offensive of 1972, when I had been in Vietnam for just a short time, I first started flying combat, but right out of the shoot, my aircraft was hit by .50-caliber enemy machine gun bullets. The bullets struck the transmission, and I started losing power and heading to the ground. I immediately went into autorotate mode to get to the ground safely and out of enemy fire. I lowered the collective, falling like a rock, just like practice. Ten feet from the ground, I flared the aircraft nose up, pulling up on the collective rotor blade, and moved from flat to sharp edge, which grabbed the air and pulled me up slowly and softly, enabling me to land on the ground without power. The instant response, without a thought, was the correct one. My gunner and I safely exited the aircraft, took cover, directed gunship fire to the enemy position, and were later picked up by another company aircraft.

The gunship pilot had a big laugh, though. Rather than try to recover my broken aircraft, the command decided, because of the great enemy concentration, to order the gunships to blow up my plane. The gunships rolled in on my ship and hit it with as many rockets as they could to make sure it was destroyed and that nothing was left to fall into enemy hands. So, I was shot down my first time out. I thought, 'This is going to be a long war.'

I got lucky another time early in my tour when taking heavy fire. After finding the enemy position near Quang Tri, I called in the gunships after my gunner dropped smoke grenades in the area. Then I started losing power (probably a shell in the engine).

I managed to maintain enough speed and altitude to get away from the jungle, where I would crash into trees that were over 60 feet tall along the beach, which was a remote area of sand.

As I approached the beach, my airspeed got down to about 50 knots (a knot is 1.151 miles per hour) when the engine quit, and I started dropping like a rock. There must have been damage to the transmission because when I attempted an auto-rotation, the main rotor blades shook and slowed down, not sped up as they should have done. At my rate of descent, I knew the landing was going to be very hard and possibly fatal. Still, I instinctively thought of a way to survive; immediate action was necessary. I pulled the aircraft up so that the tail section would hit first. When it hit, I reasoned, it would fold like an accordion, absorbing the shock of the crash.

I was right; the tail section hit first, shearing off from the fuselage. The round shape of the main fuselage was supposed to roll along the beach like a ball. (That was what I had been told when I transitioned from the UH 1, Huey, to the OH6, Loach.) The gamble paid off; the craft rolled along the beach, bouncing like a beach ball. Sand filled our eyes, ears, and noses, and the ship filled with dust and smoke. When it stopped, I climbed out, then helped my gunner exit the aircraft, which was on fire.

"How was that for a landing?" I asked.

The gunner happily remarked, "Any landing that we walk away from is a great landing."

He grabbed his 30-caliber machine gun; in the early days I was armed with only a .38, so I grabbed the box of ammo for the machine gun and we ran to the tree line, prepared in case the enemy charged at us.

It was a close call, and I received my first Air Medal for valor. There would be many close encounters to come, yet my gunner and I both made it out of Vietnam alive and uninjured.

Combat flying came as a shock following the original, sweet assignment of flying the commanders around Da Nang to meetings. The only real danger in this first job was flying the leaders to the top of Marble Mountain. It was a rather interesting landing area, on the top of a small mountain about the size of a small tennis court. Winds were always swirling and unpredictable. The landings and takeoffs were a challenge, especially with a two-star general sitting in the back seat. I continued learning and soon was no longer considered a greenhorn.

However, these trips did not do much to prepare me for combat missions at Quang Tri. I learned mostly by going out and doing it. Once out of Quang Tri, I asked the company executive officer if I could be assigned for a few days with a sister cavalry, Unit F Troop 7$^{th}$ Cav., or 4$^{th}$ Cav. The request was granted, so I started going on scout missions as an observer. When I returned to F Troop 8$^{th}$ Cav., I planned to use these learned combat techniques to get the platoon to full strength, with the combat skills we enjoyed before the loss of our experienced pilots and gunners.

Now I was the scout platoon leader, a second lieutenant in charge of 10 aircraft and 15 crew chiefs/gunners and mechanics (some great, some often high on marijuana). I was also responsible for the pilots (some with good experience, and others with none). I took command by arming all the Loaches with the M134 mini-gun (a 7.62-by-51mm NATO six-barrel machine gun) that could fire up to 2000 rounds a minute. This war machine featured Gatling-style rotation barrels with an external power source, an electric motor engaged by pressing the trigger on the cyclic.

The gunners didn't want them; they were used to handling downward fire on the enemy with their .30-caliber machine guns that hung from the right side of the aircraft on a bungee cord. However, I convinced them that when the aircraft encountered enemy fire from a tree line, it would be good to have both the mini-gun and the M60 firing back.

My next challenge was to get the lazy doper mechanics to work with the dedicated and skilled crew chiefs/gunners. These experienced men did not want to waste their time on these lowlifes. My thinking was that if they worked together, there would be much more assurance that combat casualties would come from the enemy, not from a mechanical failure in the field.

What about the pilots who were not so happy about taking orders from me, the green second lieutenant? I would quickly gain their respect. After several weeks of daily training and mixing up aircraft and crew, I devised an ingenious plan. It came from watching a movie in which the actors had to draw lots to determine who would go first in a golf game. Each morning, all the combat-ready aircraft numbers were written on separate sheets and placed in a box. The same was done with each crew chief/gunner. I would pull out the two aircraft numbers for that day's mission, along with two names of the crew chiefs/gunners. I would also assign the pilots based on the mission, their experience, and the number of hours flown that week. I often assigned myself because I had difficulty sending some of the scared pilots on these missions up north. The additional missions, however, would contribute to the slow change the war would have on my emotional state.

The changes worked; the experienced crew chiefs/gunners started working with the less-experienced and lazy teams. It seemed that marijuana use did not occur when these teams were working on aircraft together. During my time as scout platoon leader, there were no mechanical failures in a combat mission.

The crew chief/gunner had a unique relationship with the pilot. The crew chief was the mechanic for the maintenance of the aircraft and the guns on the aircraft. He would also act as the gunner on a combat mission. Most of the pilots would work with their crew chief when repairing and maintaining the aircraft; after all, they were both going to rely on the machine to get them back to base alive. The pilot was responsible for operating the aircraft and flying in such a manner so as not to get shot. This unique relationship is great as a matter of course, but it meant total and unchallenging commitment to each other –TRUST! The crew chief/gunner would work in close collaboration with all the mechanics to ensure the aircraft was combat-ready. The gunner would confirm that the M60 machine gun and the mini-gun were operating properly. We carried as much ammo on board as possible (especially for the mini-gun), as well as plenty of smoke grenades, white phosphorus grenades, C-4 explosives and even some quart cans of hydraulic fluid.

Each time the pilot and gunner took off in the morning, both knew that the day might be their last. Most days would require this team of two (with supporting force overhead) to flush out the enemy and start taking fire. The mini-gun was so loud that neither could hear the other. To return safely to base, they relied on skill, training, an inherent ability to take instant and correct action, and many times just darn good luck.

The day in, day-out conditions of combat began to take a toll on us. It was up to each soldier to maintain some bit of sanity. The worst times for me were when the crew I had sent out failed to return. The empty bunk, the lone cavalry hat hanging — the silent pain over a fallen comrade.

My solution had to come in steps because the effect of combat developed slowly, and was often unnoticed. I changed from being a leader who laughed, joked, and kicked around with guys in the mess hall or officers' club to a more private, taciturn leader. I wanted to be alone more often.

I had to make the simple decision that I would not be killed in this "stinky," rainy, smoke-ridden country. I quickly learned that I could not feel for the Vietnamese. When entering the free-fire zone, anything that moved was fair game. The village oxen, a small child, a mother getting fresh water from the creek, a wild deer or pig, a chicken, a bird — all would be shot before they could shoot back.

To survive, I had to make a complete mental separation between my team and the Vietnamese people. Why? It is that split second between life and death, that heartbeat during which to take instant, instinctive correct action. Any hesitation meant death. I could not maintain the slightest notion that I could not shoot just because the movement of the bush might be something that was NOT the enemy. If it was a free-fire zone, it was "shoot first, think later."

I did not allow myself to feel any attachment to the people, their culture, or even their struggle. I would go to the morning briefing, get the orders to search a particular area for the enemy, and do whatever it took to come home alive.

Pilots and gunners also received bullet-proof vests of standard green, but after seeing a fellow scout pilot from another unit painting a red bulls-eye on his, I decided to modify mine. I took a black marker and drew a dot on it, maybe the size of an apple. My thinking was simply this: that no one could ever hit what they were aiming at, like a bull's-eye.

This dot was funny when I drew it, but the joke would not last long. The first time enemy fire brought down my aircraft, my gunner and I ran to hide in the tall grass of the jungle, awaiting rescue. I happened to look down and see my vest with the black dot. I quickly "slugged" it into the tall grass, where it most likely remains to this day. As you can imagine, a big black dot does not have the same camouflage effect as the color green does.

In addition to these antics, there was always the fall back of a bottle of Jack Daniels. However, as the days, weeks, and months dragged on, my fear and sorrow were replaced with hatred. It would take some time after my return home for me to address this.

After a few months as scout platoon leader, I had a record of no one having been shot down or crashed. Then a new captain signed on for duty — Captain O'Burne. On his first tour, he had been an infantry "ground pounder." Then, for his second assignment, he had gone to flight school and become an Army aviator. Though I knew that O'Burne would be taking over the scout platoon I had worked hard to develop, we quickly became friends. The captain was one to be respected, and he showed immediate respect for me when he saw how the platoon operated and heard the ideas I had developed.

Our first encounter was one to remember. We went to my hutch and finished off a bottle of Jack Daniels. I grabbed a fellow pilot as a driver, and we stole the XO's Jeep. We headed to the Air Force officers' club across the runway at Da Nang. Our driver was Blue Ghost 10. We always gave Blue Ghost 10 a bad time because the number 10 had a negative connotation in Vietnam, where it was a derogatory saying. We often heard the maids say, "You bad GI, me no like you, you Number 10, you very bad GI…NUMBER 10…"

So off we went to get drunk at the officer's club at the Air Force base, not knowing Number 10 may have been drunker than we were. We finished off another bottle of Jack and praised the "fatherland" after each shot. We started drinking Matus wine, pasting the labels on our foreheads, still praising the "fatherland." We three then staggered to the Jeep and headed back to the barracks. Number 10 wanted to climb a telephone pole, so he stopped the vehicle. O'Burne and I drank some bottles of Matus wine and watched.

Finally, we yelled, "Come down, come down, Number 10! We need to get some rest for tomorrow's mission." No luck — Number 10 was too scared to come down! Since we were in the XO's Jeep, we got on the radio and called the fire department. All would have been fine and we would have gotten away with it if it hadn't been for that darn siren. Needless to say, the XO was notified. We should have been in big trouble, but the XO was drunk too! He told the firefighter to let us return with his vehicle.

The next day, I took the captain on his first scouting mission. I explained that the scout's first objective in combat was to never travel in a straight line. We always moved up and down and side to side. Though hung over, I was familiar with this type of flying, but the captain was not. I looked over at the co-pilot's seat, and there sat a sick, green captain. I saw drool dripping from the microphone attached to his helmet, and a fresh pile of vomit on the lap of the captain — who, by the way, never made a sound. I made only one remark: "To the fatherland!"

The captain swore and I flew the aircraft with the green captain to the base for refueling. I told the captain he had had enough training for one day and that he should return to barracks. My gunner and I finished the second half of the mission. That evening, of course, we partook of the "hair of the dog that bit us," but we were much calmer about it. The transition between platoon leaders went well, and we became friends for life. Much more would happen to us on missions — but one of us would walk home, while the other would be medivaced.

Vietnam was another world. We often talked about going home –returning to the "real world." Laughing, cringing, and watching each other's back kept us alive and somewhat sane. The occasional call to family and the daily letters would keep our homes alive, but not hide the truth of our fears of never returning there.

# ACTS OF VALOR

I never understood how soldiers could handle the daily struggle of combat without some way of compensating for it. When I was in Vietnam, most of us suppressed our fear by joking about killing some "gooks" or "slant eyes." Others sought protection in prayer and asking for forgiveness. Then there were those like me: the men who got drunk every night because a hangover wasn't as bad as the fear of dying.

The effectiveness of military training, however, should not be underestimated. I had a trained response for each mission and threat I faced. At the same time, there were unusual circumstances in which I could reach deep inside myself and intuitively find the right reaction. By combining my learned skills with the intuitive responses, I not only survived but was able to distinguish myself by displaying what was considered heroism under fire. I did not intend to be heroic; all I did was react at the moment. I later asked myself what the hell I'd been thinking. I could have gotten myself killed.

Nonetheless, I received awards for doing what I thought had to be done. Each medal or award came with a narrative of what had happened or what I had done to deserve the recognition. These descriptions do not come close to describing what actually happened. They leave out the real agony of war, highlighting only the "bravery."

It is impossible to put into words the devastating sounds, smells, and sights that can develop in a millisecond. But my memories are vivid, often taking the form of dreams or flashbacks. They spring to mind when something I see, hear, or smell evokes the memory — sometimes for just a moment, sometimes longer.

There are so many memories: the piercing staccato of machine gun fire; the ear-splitting whiz of rockets, and the frantic yelling all still come to life in my mind's eye. Rockets from the gunships fired at the enemy's position to help protect our aircraft. Yells or orders over the radio are telling gunships at the location to lay down their fire. Flashes from the barrels of our machine guns. The blinding explosion of rockets, the thick smoke of the grenades dropped to mark enemy positions. The smells of burning foliage or the wood around the bunker. Other smells too unspeakable to identify.

The descriptions in the award citations did not mention the smoke from gunpowder that seeped into every pore of my body, mixing with the sweat and tears. The deafening cracks as each bullet left the end of the machine gun that my gunner wheeled out of the side of the craft. Feeling the twisting and turning of the aircraft, with the flap-flap-flap of the rotor blades. Pulling the plane up and down, side to side, to dodge the bullets as they whizzed by, some piercing the skin of the helicopter and missing us by inches.

When we were back at camp, we would count the holes. Once we counted more than 20, one right through the front canopy, head high, continuing through the back of my seat and lodged in the back near the transmission. I must have leaned over to look out just as the bullet was fired at me. Bending over at that instant saved my life!

I recall hearing the hundreds of rounds spitting from the mini-gun as the barrels rotated so fast I saw not six barrels but only one great one, spraying havoc at 2000 rounds a minute. How does one forget the sounds and intensity of the radio communications directing fire to the enemy position? Or the familiar words, "Taking fire!" Then there were the communications on the intercom in the aircraft between my gunner and me, the shouts and screams pointing out enemy fire positions, all the while looking to see how I could fly this plane to safety as well as accomplish our mission to find and kill the enemy. The adrenaline rush was unlike anything I had ever felt, at least until the next mission. One major issue was developing: I found myself craving this adrenaline and accepting more missions than I needed to fly.

I soon realized that the adrenaline high was addictive and often made me act with a reckless disregard for my life, my gunner's life, or the life of the enemy. The intensity of the moment was all that mattered: kill these little bastards — kill the gook sons o' bitches.

There is no way of explaining how I felt when I received medals for valor or heroism. I would just thank whichever commander or general showed up to present it.

One of our pilots received an award. When we were on a mission, we joked about it. Over the radio, I'd say, "Blue Ghost 10, can I touch your medal? Do you shine it every night? I wish I were a hero like you! Do you lock it up at night?"

Blue Ghost 16 (our commander) would interrupt, saying, "That is enough — the awards are to be respected."

Then came the great joke. That is a joke for us that have used radios on aircraft to communicate. Usually one would say, "This is Blue Ghost 17, requesting to land." Response from the tower would be granted land runway 15. However, when there is a communication uttered on the radio without identifying the speaker (i.e. Blue Ghost 17) the here is what you get

> "Who dat." "Who dat who say who dat — who dat who say who dat after dat…"

Blue Ghost 16, then commands, "That is enough!"

Here are some awards I received. I have included the words on the citation, but I explain what actually happened.

My second Air Medal for Valor came when I trained with a sister unit because all the senior pilots had been killed and I was to take over as scout platoon leader. I got permission from the CO to fly with them, so I could learn their techniques, then come back and train our green pilots.

I went on a couple of missions. The first sortie resulted in our getting shot down, but we landed safely. The next mission I served as co-pilot; I was supposed to be observing the tactics so that I could go back to my unit and teach those tactics to the new pilots. We got shot down again; this was not the lesson I intended to learn.

That flight resulted in being awarded by first metal for Heroism, as well as my first purple heart.

General Orders         "NGUY HIEM"
30 October 1972:

Number 3192

### AWARD OF THE AIR MEDAL FOR HEROISM

Tc 4391: The following awards are announced,

F Troop, 4$^{th}$ Air Cav.

Award: Air Medal Second Award with "V" Device

Date of Service: 18 June 1972

Theater: Republic of Vietnam

Authority: By direction of the President under the provisions of Executive Order 9158, 11 May 1942, as amended by Executive Order 9242-A, 11 September 1942, AR 672-5-1 and USARV Supplement 1 to AR 672-5-1 dated 10 August 1970.

Reason:

For heroism, while engaged in aerial flight in connection with military operations against a hostile force: First Lieutenant distinguished himself by exceptionally valorous actions while serving as copilot/observer on a light observation helicopter on a reconnaissance mission. Lieutenant's helicopter was taken under intense, large caliber machine gun, automatic weapons, and small arms fire. Lieutenant marked the area for Cobra gunships, as his suppressive fires raked the enemy positions enabling both the lead and his own ship to exit the area. Returning to the same area a short while later to make an artillery strike damage assessment, the lead ship was taken under a devastating crossfire ambush. Again raking the enemy positions with highly accurate suppressive fires, Lieutenant's helicopter flew through the ambush in order to cover the lead ship. Noticing that his aircraft was going down, Lieutenant calmly kept firing into enemy positions until his aircraft was clear of the enemy stronghold. On the ground, he assisted the pilot in shutting the aircraft down despite sporadic hostile small arms fire. His actions were in keeping with the highest traditions of the military service and reflect great credit upon himself, his unit, and the United States Army.

Though the author got some of the details right, he left out the worst ones, and there is no indication of the intensity of the encounter. The truth is that we made a crash landing; the tail rotor hit the ground first. I thought we had landed on our skids, so I unsnapped my harness and seatbelt as the cabin filled with smoke. However, when we hit on our main skids, I was thrown out of the plane. After landing on the sand, I tried to push myself up, but the next thing I remembered was being wheeled on a gurney from a Medevac helicopter to a field hospital. I was later told that as I pushed myself off the sand, after flying through the air to the ground, the main rotor blade was still spinning and bouncing and struck me in the head, slicing through my helmet. The doctor said if the blade had been an inch lower, my head would have been cut off. I only said that it did not seem to be my time, saved by luck once again! So, I received my first Purple Heart as well as the Air Medal for Valor.

I left Vietnam with 16 air medals, two more for valor. I think, as a matter of course, pilots get one air medal for every 50 or so hours of combat missions, unless one is given for valor.

Though there were intense moments it wasn't until September that I had to take immediate action. I would receive an award for those actions. My thoughts, however, was to do what I could to save a fellow pilot.

The Award read:


GENERAL ORDER             "NGUY HIEM"
24 January 1973

Number 260

<u>AWARD OF THE DISTINGUISHED FLYING CROSS</u>

TC 4391: The following AWARD is announced.

F Trp, 8th Cav (WGZOAA) APO SF 96388 FA

Awarded: Distinguished Flying Cross

Date of Service: 30 September 1972

Theater: Republic of Vietnam

Authority: By direction of the President under the provisions of Executive Order 9158, 11 May 1942, as amended by Executive Order 9242-A, 11 September 1942, AR 672-5-1 and USARV Supplement 1 to AR 672-5-1 dated 10 August 1970.

Reason:

>For heroism, while engaged in aerial flight in connection with military operations against a hostile force: First Lieutenant distinguished himself by exceptionally valorous actions while serving as pilot of light observation helicopter during a scout and recon mission west of the city of Mo Duc, the Republic of Vietnam. First Lieutenant's trail helicopter reported receiving fire and was going down. First Lieutenant circled behind the crippled aircraft and directed the Cobra gunships to the enemy's position. After the damaged aircraft had crashed in a rice paddy, Lieutenant maneuvered his aircraft to a dike to pick up the downed crewmen who had exited their aircraft and were running for cover. Following the pick-up, Lieutenant flew his aircraft out

of the area to safety. Lieutenant's actions were in keeping with the highest traditions of the military service and reflect great credit upon himself, his unit, and the United States Army.

The description depicts the basic event, but does not explain the unbelievable loud noise of machine gun firing, rockets blasting, and the frantic calls, "taking fire." Blue Ghost 10 was my tail gunner on that day and on our second leg of the mission we encountered a newly constructed bunker. There were also several fox holes around the bunker with enemy riflemen in them, protected by gunny sacks filled with dirt. I was flying down a trail that look as though it had been heavily traveled when I spotted the camouflaged structure on the side of the trail in the jungle. My gunner started firing at the location, then we noticed the outer fox holes with enemy AK 47. Then all hell broke out. I was dodging flying shells, some hitting my aircraft. My trail loach was firing at the enemy positions as well, and all yelling "taken fire." Then the dreaded sound of "I'm hit, I'm hit" came from my trail loach. Again, "I'm hit but ok to land come and get me." I quickly responded, "Got you covered, get out of the area." I keep my aircraft between the firing enemy gun positions and the trail loach. We marked the enemy positions a close a possible with smoke and headed out of the area. Blue Ghost 10 was able to safely land his aircraft in a rice paddy out of enemy firing range. The gunships were pounding on the enemy positions while I landed and picked up the wounded pilot and his gunner flying to where the medivac helicopter was waiting.

I flew back to bases picked up another pilot and returned where the downed aircraft was landed. Jumped in cranked it up and flew the aircraft out of the area. The injured pilot and the downed aircraft were returned.

All the free drinks at the officer's club that night did not help my increasing problem with getting drunk every night.

As time went by my skills were improving, I was able to find the enemy, engage, get out of there and let the gunships to their jobs, until once again in November, I was called upon to take action to protect and save another injured pilot.

My first reaction was, damned it, it seems like I just had to do the same thing a couple of months ago.

The award read:

GNERAL ORDERS     "NGUY KOEM"  21 December 1972

## AWARD OF THE ARMY COMMENDATION MEDAL FOR HEROISM

TC 439  The following AEARD is announced.

Awarded: Army Commendation Medal (First Oak Leaf Cluster) with "V" device

Date of service:  24 November 1972

Theater: Republic of Vietnam

Authority: By direction of the Secretary of the Army under

        Under the provisions of  Ar 672-5-1 and USARV     Supplement 1 to Ar 672-5-1 dated 10 August 1970

Reason:

> For heroism in connection with military operations against a hostel force: First Lieutenant

distinguished himself by exceptional valorous actions while serving as pilot of a light observation helicopter. During an Air Cavalry visual reconnaissance mission northeast of the city f Tay-Ninh, the flight came under enemy fire with the trail aircraft pilot being severely wounded. Lieutenant began to cover his trail aircraft as they left the hostile area. When the wounded pilot decided to land the aircraft rather than return to the airfield, Lieutenant landed beside the downed pilot for the pickup and returned him for medical care. Lieutenant then returned to the landing site on another aircraft and flew the damaged aircraft out of the area. Through Lieutenant's actions, the wounded pilot received medical care without delay and a damaged aircraft was recovered from a hostile area. Lieutenant's actions were in keeping with the highest traditions of the military service and reflect great credit upon himself, his unit and the United States Army.

I initially thought that it was going to be a long war, but I wondered why the enemy could not hit me. The exact same thing happened two months earlier near a city of MoDuc when my tail gunner got hit and I dodged the bullets. There seemed to be much more intense enemy fire on this rescue, however.

My recollection of that day is much more intense. Another scout aircraft and I were on a typical hunter-killer mission. We had two Cobra gunships flying high above, as well as a Huey command ship with our commander and a village representative. The command ship was making sure the scout reconnaissance was in the right area. If we engaged, it would make sure friendly troops were not in the area. On this particular mission, the scouts followed trails or paths in the jungle that appeared to be packed or fresh. I was leading with the second aircraft close behind when machine gun fire from the ground broke out. I started taking fire from a machine gun concealed in a camouflaged bunker. Captain O'Burne, the pilot of the trail Loach, yelled over the radio, "Machine gun nest at your 2 o'clock," so I veered to avoid the bullets. However, the trail Loach could not turn in time, and the machine gun bullets ripped through the front of the aircraft, taking off the top of Captain O'Burne's right foot, His cockpit was covered with blood as he attempted to maneuver out of the way. I had my gunner throw a smoke grenade to mark the approximate location of the bunker. The gunships started laying down fire in the area. Captain O'Burne was moving out of the area, and I was close behind. I kept talking to Blue Ghost 15, asking how he was doing and if he could maintain control of the aircraft. He explained that he was going into shock and might pass out. His gunner climbed out of the back of the craft, slid along the outside of the aircraft, and took the co-pilot's seat to the left of the injured pilot. The gunner took out the sawed-off broomstick and placed it in the cavity of the co-pilot controls. We had often rehearsed that method to land in an emergency like this. The gunner took control of the aircraft and informed us on the radio that Captain O'Burne had just slumped over, but was being held up by his harness and seat belt. The gunner landed the helicopter safely in a rice paddy. Enemy bullets whistled over the downed aircraft, and I maneuvered my aircraft between the downed plane and the machine gun nest. My gunner started laying fire on their position with his M60, and I kept squeezing bursts from the mini-gun. The constant rocket attack of the Cobra gunship, as well as our firing at the bunker, finally silenced the enemy. I moved in behind the downed aircraft, and my gunner and the other gunner carried Captain O'Burne to my plane and put him in the back. O'Burne's gunner took off his own shirt and wrapped the captain's foot to stop the bleeding. I headed out of the combat area and rendezvoused with a medivac helicopter that had the personnel to care for O'Burne while flying to the field hospital. Captain O'Burne would be sent home.

I returned to base camp and grabbed another pilot to fly me back to the combat area to retrieve the downed aircraft. South Vietnamese ground forces had entered the area and secured the plane. I was to fly it out of the area. I climbed into the front seat to start it up when something made me stop and think. I knew that often ground troops would prepare a downed helicopter to be taken out of the field by lowering a sling from a Huey, lifting the aircraft, and getting it back to base camp. When that occurred, it would require the ground troops to climb to the main rotor and unlatch the metal snaps holding the pins that kept the rotor blades on the central hub. I had had the same eerie feeling years before when I was under the backhoe on the ranch, trying to repair a clogged fuel pump. I had heard the slight crack and pulled myself from under the machine less than a second before the backhoe fell. When this same feeling overtook me, I got out of the aircraft, climbed up the main rotor connection, and checked the latches. Sure enough, one of the latches had been pulled up. If I had started the engine, the blade with the loose lock would have flown off. The other three rotor blades would have sliced through the aircraft and chopped me in half.

When I hit the officers' club that night and talked about my experience at the ranch and the close call with the loose latch, I got a few extra drinks — it was a day to remember. I still do not know if one of the ground troops had attempted to sabotage the aircraft, or was just making preparations to sling the plane out. In any event, after finding the latch lifted, I examined the entire aircraft with a fine-tooth comb before starting it up and flying back to safety. I was able to get Blue Ghost 15 and his gunner to safety and save an aircraft. For that, I received the award.

All missions were going well, no crashes or fellow pilots and gunners getting killed. Then of course, there is the volunteer.

I had seen enough war movies to know not to volunteer, but me and a couple of buddies decided to help out. That would result in being awarded another metal.

The Citation read:

GENERAL ORDERS  "NGUY HIEM"  15 December 1972

NUMBER  3821

### AWARD OF THE ARMY COMMENDATION MEDAL

Award:  Army Commendation Medal

Dates of Service: 15 December 1972

Theater: Republic of Vietnam

Authority:

By direction of the President under the provisions of Executive Order 9158, 11 May 1942, as amended by Executive Order 9242-A, 11 September 1942, AR 672-5-1 and USARV Supplement 1 to AR 672-5-1 dated 10 August 1970.

Organization: F Trp, 8$^{th}$ Air Cav

Reason: For meritorious service in connection with military operations against a hostile force.

I have no idea what an award for meritorious service means, but here is what we did. Three other pilots, four crew chiefs, and I volunteered to farrier, or fly together, our four aircraft from Quan Tri to Pu Bai, south of Hue in central Vietnam. The trip required us to stay overnight in an outpost of the Southern Vietnam army. We worried about whether or not these soldiers were on our side because we had learned not to trust anyone. In any event, in the early morning, the camp came under a shelling or rocket attack. Rocket attacks are alarming. When the rockets would start hitting the compound, I never knew where the next would hit. All I could do was make it into a bunker or at least crawl under something. I recall squeezing into the culvert under the road. We then realized that the aircraft were in danger and that we should do something before they were destroyed. We quickly started the crafts, then lifted off in different directions to find where the shells were coming from. Another aircraft located the enemy gun and called in friendly artillery fire to silence the weapons. It worked; the firing stopped. I don't know if our guns knocked them out or if the enemy simply pulled the gun back into the cave to use on another day. But at least for that day they had stopped.

Another reason for our joint decision to get into the air was that it was not unusual, after a rocket attack, to encounter a ground attack. Many an outpost was overrun that way. That was scary because, as officers, we were equipped with only a .38 revolver — not a fair match against AK-47 automatic rifles, the preferred weapon of the enemy. No ground attack came. Our flying over the region looking for the enemy may have changed their mind. We were all awarded the Army Commendation Medal.

As my skills were improving, and I was lucky enough not to get shot or killed in February, my commander put me in for my final medal: The Bronze Star.

GENERAL ORDERS        "NGUY HIEM"
27 January 1973

## AWARD OF THE BRONZE STAR MEDAL

Award:  Bronze Star Medal

Dates of Service: 5 Feb 73

Theater: Republic of Vietnam

Authority:

By direction of the President under the provisions of Executive Order 9158, 11 May 1942, as amended by Executive Order 9242-A, 11 September 1942, AR 672-5-1 and USARV Supplement 1 to AR 672-5-1 dated 10 August 1970.

Organization: F Trp, 8$^{th}$ Air Cav

Reason: For meritorious service in connection with military operations against a hostile force.


My commander told me this award was for my being shot down three times and surviving. Twice I was able to pull my injured crew chief or wounded pilot from the damaged aircraft to safety, or at least help them to the tree line for cover until help arrived. I was the craziest scout pilot he had ever seen.

I must admit, hiding in the bushes for a few hours while gunship and enemy ground troops exchanged fire was no fun. There was always the fear that the enemy might capture the downed pilot and his gunner and take them to a POW camp. This fear was everyone's secret fear, but no one admitted it. And yes, I was a crazy scout pilot, but at least I didn't come home in a box!

The images of war are impossible to erase completely, but there were some events that had elements of humor, which helped us stay sane. For example, one day I found myself in the middle of a combat zone. As usual, I would fly four feet from the ground, looking for the enemy. Typically, I would scout the edges of the area I wanted to examine. This time, three enemy machine guns opened fire at each corner of the triangle. I must have flown over a camouflaged enemy machine gun. Everywhere I turned, I was getting fired upon. If I tried to lift up, I got fire from all three corners. My ears were ringing. My mouth, nose, and eyes were filled with gunpowder. My gunner was firing the M60 machine gun hanging on the bungee cord above his door; I was squeezing the trigger on the mini-gun hanging on the left side of the helicopter, spitting out 2000 rounds a minute.

It was hard to talk to each other on the intercom because of the thunderous noise. My gunner and I were yelling and screaming about the locations of the guns, and trying to direct our return fire. We were in a panic and could not focus. The only thing going through my mind was, "We are going to die in this damned place."

Unexpectedly, we heard a calm voice over the radio, overpowering our frantic cries of desperation. I recognized the voice as that of a 19-year-old gunship pilot "covering" me. This young pilot calmly reminded me that I'd bought a new alarm watch that had arrived in the mail that very morning. He knew I'd decided to leave it in my hutch and to not wear it in combat. He went on to say that he believed the chances of my getting out of the ambush and machine gun fire alive looked grim. He asked if he could have my new watch if I did not make it back.

Over the radio, we all laughed. Then the gunship pilot fired two rockets that exploded on one of the enemy's positions. I lowered the nose of the aircraft and headed straight over that enemy, where the other two enemy gun positions couldn't shoot at me. As we flew over the area, guns ablaze, my gunner dropped homemade bombs and smoke grenades to mark the location for further rocket launches.

Because I am able to write about this episode, you know that we were able to fly to safety. These are the kinds of happy outcomes I recalled whenever I found myself in an unhappy situation later on. And… the gun pilot got my alarm watch!

The medals now hang in a beautiful case on my wall, and remind me of that part of my life. I work hard to remember only the fun times and the joyous days of bonding with my comrades. It was the stupid acts that each of us would talk about while drinking and hiding our fears. Each pilot had remarkable stories of what had happened on any particular day. Some were true, and some were exaggerated, as mine became as the whiskey flowed. Remembering the funny things helped, but the images of war are impossible to erase completely.

The medals now hang in a beautiful case on my wall, and remind me of that part of my life.

## COWBOY VS WARRIOR?

As my memories accumulated, I formed a genuine conviction that there is one major struggle between being a cowboy and being a warrior. As a cowboy, I learned to "cowboy up" when things went bad: when a horse or steer kicked me, when I got bucked off a horse, or when I smashed my finger with the wrench while tightening a bolt. I was not supposed to let those little things bother me. But after my war days, this learned response caused me to keep the hardships of war bottled up. I became an aggressive combat pilot who took extra missions so that I would not have to order other pilots to go out. I often stressed over the loss of comrades, or over killing that one "enemy" who might have been just a poor farmer in the wrong place.

One duty haunted me for years. I was ordered to scout an area where the Air Force had dropped an "Ark-light" (blanket-bombing a particular sector). It was not a seek-and-destroy mission; it was just an attempt to make a body count in the bombed-out field so that the brass could report on the effectiveness of the explosions. It supposedly meant counting intact bodies, but usually there were body parts strewn about. My gunner and I would joke about how many pieces should be considered a full body. The black humor did not hide the fact that we were "following orders" and completing the assignment, no matter how distressing it was. Nor did the joking keep me from brushing off these terrible experiences. I would "cowboy up" and "brush it off" by hitting the bottle and staying drunk as long as possible.

What a relief when I finally let those secrets out. Writing this book is one of the ways I accomplished that!

There were so many firefights — so many instances of being fired upon or shooting back into the tree line, not knowing if we were hitting innocent farmers. So many times we made homemade bombs to throw at suspected enemy positions, to see if they would shoot at us. It all started taking its toll on me. I became more isolated and drank even more.

Halfway through my tour, I went on a wonderful R&R in Hawaii

with my wife, but that didn't help. She commented on how I no longer had any patience with anyone and would lose my temper at the drop of a hat.

Even after returning home, I had a difficult time because of my heavy drinking. Luckily, my determination to finish the instructor pilot course forced me to keep my boozing under control, but it would take several years to get rid of those pent-up emotions.

What helped was working hard to get through law school. During law school, Linda and I were fortunate enough to have a baby boy, and baby girl. Brian Elton and Carrie Ann.

When not working or studying taking care of them was a joy and distraction from memories.

Then came the demands of being a country lawyer, with hours on the road as a public defender. I did get some satisfaction from helping people. All these events help me cope.

One telltale event that exposed my dark, hidden sorrows occurred when we went to Washington D.C. and visited the Vietnam Memorial. I found the names of some of my lost fellow pilots on the wall; seeing those names brought me to tears. When my children asked if I was okay, I said, "No, this is tough and is bringing back a lot of sadness." I can still see the unhappiness in the eyes of my kids and wife. They finally knew what I had been hiding, and how the war had affected my life. When I told my daughter and son that I had put this event in this book, they said that they remembered the day clearly — that day was the first time they ever saw me cry.

I would like to present you with a poem that has just now come to mind as I write this. The sky is what I turned to in times of sorrow.

### WHY THE SKY

The mountain ridges
Cut the Sky
Changing its colors, blending
and turning
The Sky
The clouds dance and float
In the Sky
The sun and moon fight for
Equal time in the Sky
Why the Sky
It lets us breathe

A tumbleweed lifts into
The Sky
A dust devil twists and rolls
Higher and Higher
in the Sky
Why the Sky
It lets us feel

That sandy windstorm
Blocks the Sky
A moving rainstorm
Darken the Sky
The diamond stars sparkle
In the Sky
Why the Sky
It gives us joy

The birds act as though
They own the Sky
But
When lightning crashes
We know there is only one
Owner of the Sky
Leaves and loose grass move
Here and there in the Sky
Why the Sky
It
Gives us Love

An airplane darts this way
and that
Borrowing space
In the Sky
The wind moves all items
That are loose one place
Or another
In the Sky
A sunset a sunrise
Paints the Sky
Why the Sky
It reminds us
That we are but a speck
In the scheme of things

When the clouds and wind
Torment the Sky, it changes colors
When the sun, stars, and moon
Appear in the Sky
the Sky willingly
joins their dance by day and night
Why the Sky
it leads us through life


When I was a young cowboy, I always found joy and love for life in the splendor of the open range and the massive expansion of the horizon. Each day or night, the view would make me feel exactly like the words of this inspiring poem. When I was stressed, looking to the heavens at night or day always calmed me. However, as a warrior, I remember only terrible things coming from the skies. Each day I would look down from the heavens to seek out the enemy position. I used all the means at my disposal to get them to show themselves. Sometimes I dropped homemade bombs into the foliage or fired my mini-gun recklessly into the undergrowth, not caring if a woman or child was heading to the creek for water. I once killed several oxen who happened to be grazing in the free-fire zone.

Time passed at a snail's pace: days, weeks, months. I no longer wanted to gaze into the sky as I had done so many years before as a young cowboy. This significant change and hard reality showed me what war could do to a nature-loving cowboy. It would take half a lifetime for me to love the sky again.
Then there was the "why are we here" factor. I had to constantly reassure myself that I was fighting to make the world a better place — to stop Communism in its tracks.

During my R&R in Hawaii, no one knew, nor wanted to know, what was happening. Having college kids yell at me and call me "baby killer" did not help.
The lack of concern about the war and the hurtful comments saddened me as I thought of my many fallen comrades. At least they would not have to know that it appeared as though they had died for nothing.

One of my worst struggles was participating in the religious ceremony whenever a fellow pilot or gunner was killed. I would listen to the chaplain explain how "God works in mysterious ways," or how "God is on our side." I remember thinking that our enemies over the hill were probably saying the same thing about their fallen comrades. Is there an answer? I have not found one to this day!

I will state that I never lost focus or purpose. I remained a patriot, knowing we were there for a real purpose, and that many people's lives would be better because of it. However, when our unit was finally disbanded and all of us were ordered back home to new assignments, a void was left in me as Vietnam fell to the North and Communism did, in fact, spread.

The belief that the spread of Communism was something wrong has gotten lost since then. Look at our relations today with China — the same country that sent advisors to assist the North Vietnamese. Well, the same thing happened with Japan after the Second World War, and Japan is now one of our greatest allies.

Remember at the start of this book, when I reminded you not to take life too seriously? I still don't.

# RETURN TO BASE

Commencing one's day with the command "Start your aircraft" can rattle one's nerves. Fly for a couple of hours, refuel, fly another couple of hours, refuel, then out again. But this time, we spot movement and they shoot at us — contact! Mark the area with smoke, get out of there, and let the gunships do their job. Or let the South Vietnamese troops move into the area and surround the enemy. Then it's music to the ears: "Return to base!" We head to the airfield, always flying low and looking for any enemy movement. Then we land and secure our aircraft. We look over the plane for any bullet holes or damage, then turn it over to maintenance to prepare the craft for the next day's mission.

I walk to my room, and there on my bed are letters from home. I pour a glass of whiskey. I put my flight suit in the laundry box for the girls to wash and lie on the bed to read the letters.

The words from my wife or my grandmother often bring tears to my eyes because I know they are so far away, and I often have a haunting feeling that I may not ever go home. But it passes. I sit down and write a couple of letters to my wife and my grandmother, my uncle and my mom. I have another glass of whiskey and head to our makeshift officers' club. After a couple of beers, I ask if there are any poker games going on. "Yeah, at Captain O'Berne's hootch." I head over with a six-pack of beer and a bottle of Jack Daniels.

The game is on. I'm broke, so I sign a couple of "IOUs." We play for a couple of hours; then we decide to just drink.

I had one quirk. I would not leave a poker game unless I had an outstanding "IOU." I don't know why; maybe I thought I would not die if I owed someone money. That quirk was just as bad as the one a fellow pilot had. He refused to go on a mission unless he had a "green" smoke grenade hanging on the makeshift hook he affixed to the entrance of his aircraft. Each of us had our "superstitions," but we usually didn't tell anyone about them.

Then there was the payoff to the mail clerk. Every pilot took turns paying the mail clerk for information when one of our fellow pilots got a "care package" from home. For example, my grandpa, Elton (a former gunner on a bomber during the Second World War), would send me a package filled with booze and canned food like sardines, chili, jams, and beef jerky. When the mail clerk told us who had gotten a "care package," a half dozen of us would watch the recipient try to sneak quietly out of the officer's club to go to his hootch and "scarf up the goodies." After he had reached his room, we would creep down the hall, burst in, grab him, and tie him up. He would kick and fight, but there were usually at least six of us, so his struggle was useless. Then we would all look for the hidden treasure. Once we found it, we would start eating all his food and drinking his booze. Eventually we would untie him, and he would join in. He couldn't cry about it too much because most likely he had done the same thing to another pilot a week earlier.

Most nights were spent partying at our make-shift officers' club. We hired local gals to wait tables. It was part of the Vietnameses culture, when visiting in a group to "squawt" in a circle while they visited. We, however, cruelly refused to let them in our club. They would call us "number 10" but then follow our rule, afraid of losing their jobs.We even created a little kitchen area and hired a cook. We'd have burgers, hot dogs, chili, and sometimes a stew. Anything was better than the mess hall. Often we would drink and play hearts, spades, and other card games for hours upon hours, or until we got so drunk we couldn't see the cards.

Once a month, the officers stole all the steaks from the mess hall for our Air Calarly Party. Just another excuse to stay drunk all night. At the party, there would be arm-wrestling or the occasional fist fight. Sometimes, someone would through water to wet tarps and lay them across a couple of tables put together. That would be the landing area on an aircraft carrier so we would all take turns running up, jumping on the wet table belly first and fligh of the end. That amounted to doing a carrier landing with our bodies. Some fell off and bloodied their noses.

Anyone was free game for a joke. On one occasion, we all lowered our pants, bent over, and showed our bare butts (better known as mooned) a visiting colonel – who, by the way, had been warned ahead of time. It turned out to be ok because he was as drunk as most of us were.

I also recall, after such a gala, a newbie warrant officer approached me and indicated that I should apologize to him. I asked why. He said that I had "pissed" on him. I stated that I had no recollection of the event. He said that he had walked up to me to ask a question and I had turned and pissed on him. I said, "Well it's evident that I was taking a leak and when I turned, you obviously got the brunt of it all." I apologized, but suggested that he refrain from walking behind a man when he was standing next to a bush at a Cav party. It wasn't long before this young pilot got it and made a fool of himself as we all did.

Whatever happened the night before, the morning always started with a briefing by the XO. He would allow the wearing of sunglasses if necessary. At the conclusion of the briefing, when I was platoon leader, I would go to the maintenance shop and draw the names of the gunners for the day's mission and the aircraft to be used. I would check the flight logs for the pilots who would be assigned to that day's task. If I was not flying that day, I often worked with the crew chiefs and learned more about repairing the aircraft or cleaning the M60's or mini-gun. I would also go to the flight line when the aircraft returned for refueling and help the gun pilots re-arm the craft with rockets and bullets for their machine guns. I would check on whether the scouts had enough concussion grenades, smoke grenades, white phosphorus grenades, and homemade bombs. Then off they went on their second leg.

I preferred being on a mission to staying on the flight line. I always worried about sending the gunner and pilot out and then learning that they had crashed and been killed in action. There was absolutely nothing I could do about it. I would often go to the command shack and listen on the radio to the activity. It was quite a sight to see all of us huddled around the radio, listening, especially when contact was made. We'd hear the gunships confirm that they had seen the smoke where the enemy was located and were directing rocket fire to that location. We would hear the scouts yelling, "Taking fire at two o'clock." We would hear the command ship tell the scouts to get the hell out of there and let the gunship blast the hell out of the enemy.

When the planes returned to base, we would often meet them with cheers and sometimes a bottle of whiskey. Laughs and hugs were abundant — except when there was a missing aircraft or when the medivac ship was bringing in the wounded crew. We would help put them in an ambulance to the field hospital. Luckily, this did not happen often.

It was remarkable how camaraderie developed between the gunners and the pilots, especially the scout platoon. We would show our genuine caring for their fears and sorrows. Still, some of us held back because we did not want to get too close to them and cause ourselves greater pain if they were killed. When replacements checked in, we were friendly but would not "buddy up" quickly.

I often checked on the "newbies" in their barracks (or, as we called them, their "hootches") to see how they were coping with being away from home. I would work with them on maintenance. These joint efforts often created flashbacks to my days working in the shop at the ranch, or at Coaldale. It was difficult trying to be friendly yet keeping my distance.

The commander would often hire local showgirls and bands to entertain the troops in the hangers. Some of the "drunken gang" would get on stage and dance and sing with them, especially when they were murdering an American song. What a joy to have a little bit of home brought to us.

I was fortunate enough to go to Saigon and see the USO show when Ann-Margret was there, as well as to see one of Bob Hope's last shows. We flew over with the medivac crew, so we were given front-row seats. The rest of the unit was stuck in the nosebleed section. The show was one of the highlights of my tour. Fantastic entertainment and a piece of home!

On our off time, we would sometimes take a Jeep and go to the restaurants in downtown Saigon. It was about a half hour from our base, so we didn't need a pass or leave. Sometimes we would pick up supplies from the supply depot and get two birds with one stone. There was a "not-too-bad" Mexican restaurant in Saigon. Though there were also a lot of little shops, I did not want to buy anything. I did not want to get to know the culture or the way the Vietnamese were trying to make a living. That was the saddest part of my tour — keeping myself isolated from the culture and people, even the "friendlies." I did not want to have a second of hesitation to kill someone if I had to. I felt that seeing them as animals, as less than real people, would keep me alive. These are some of the terrible things I regret, even to this day. I know now of the deep kindness that the Vietnamese people have. How they care for their families and friends, and their clean, healthy food that I refused to eat when I was in their country, but now enjoy often.

I have regrets about the way I acted and the terrible things I was forced to do. I can't disregard, however, that those actions or conduct may have allowed me to keep my word and not die in that "damned" place.

Not unlike troops in any other war, we combat soldiers were a strange lot. We consistently found ways to overcome the nagging thought of getting killed, maimed, or crippled. As I write, I remember all the difficult choices I made and the many actions I took to survive. The questions still linger in my mind: Did I really have to do all that? Did I go too far? Was I too quick to shoot? Maybe then I would not have killed the innocent farmer or oxen.

I have not found the answer, nor do I know another combat soldier who has answered similar questions. These are the queries that spark my memories even today, over 45 years after the event.

What is rewarding now are memories of my law cases, such as when I was able to prove that my client did not commit the crime of which he or she was accused. The pleasure in representing those client who wanted to adopt a child replaced the sad memories. Also, the diversity of cases like battling over mining claims or breach of contract disputes or even divorces kept me active and away from thoughts of the past.

At the end of the day, during a trial the words "we will reconvene in the morning" would replace the familiar words, "return to base."

# HIDING TRUTHS

I was a green combat pilot, fresh out of training, wanting to be a patriot. In military, high school, the staff instilled a patriotic spirit in us. The four-year Reserve Officer Training Course (ROTC) at the university reinforced that patriotism. Even though the peace movement was at its height in the late 1960s and early 1970s, as a philosophy major, I had all the beautiful, peace-loving, attractive chicks as classmates, but once I had to wear my uniform to class, that ruined my love life. Still, I remained a patriot; I was willing to go to war if that was what the president required.

So, from college life to flight school life to Vietnam life. I went to war as a well-meaning, starry-eyed patriot, but doing and seeing what I did challenged every ounce of that patriotism.

To maintain what I thought was patriotism, I would use derogatory, offensive words: gooks, chinks, or slant-eyes. I soon stopped caring about life. "Shoot no matter what — get those the little bastards" became a battle cry. I would try to kill them at every chance.

On one occasion, I flew down a road, chasing a "gook" just as he dove into a grass hut. I told my gunner to drop a white phosphorus hand grenade so that it would roll into the hut and kill everyone inside when it exploded. The grenade was dropped perfectly; it entered the doorway. The door closed and the hut was demolished after the explosion. We both laughed at our accomplishment. To this day I regret my actions, knowing there may have been women and children in there.

On another occasion, a "chink" kept emerging from a cave and shooting at my aircraft. I got mad, landed the helicopter, frictioned or tightened down all the controls, and told my gunner to cover me with his machine gun. I jumped out of my aircraft, ran to the entrance of the cave, and pitched two white phosphorus grenades inside it. How dumb and reckless I was becoming. At any time, the man inside could have popped out and shot me. I didn't care; I just wanted to get him.

Then there was the day when my trail scout and I were bored. After we had located the enemy, we flew to a safe area, waiting for our next mission. I spotted a man riding down the road on a bicycle with an attached trailer. I radioed my trail Loach: "Doesn't that look like enemy transport?" We laughed and agreed that something should be done. I told my gunner to spray a few rounds next to the bicycle and see what happened. The cyclist jumped off and ran into the forest. Over the radio, I said, "Yep, he has to be the enemy driving an enemy vehicle because he ran when shot at him! We must destroy the vehicle." I insisted that the destruction be executed with precision. I suggested that each aircraft take turns having its gunner drop a grenade in such a way that it would roll down the road and under the "enemy vehicle."

I, in the lead Loach, went first. I flew along the road and told my gunner when to drop his grenade. Damn it; it bounced past the vehicle. The trail Loach tried, and his grenade landed closer, but not all the way under the enemy vehicle.

We went back and forth until each aircraft was almost out of grenades. Finally, I got my gunner to drop it at the exact moment. The grenade bounced completely under the bike and its trailer and blew them up. The problem was, I had become so intent on winning the contest, I had slowed our aircraft to almost a hover directly over the enemy vehicle. The debris from the explosion of bike parts flew into the air — handlebars, wheels, spokes, and all. The handlebar crashed through the fiberglass front of the aircraft, shattering it. Parts got caught in the pedals that controlled the tail rotor. Without a functioning tail rotor, and when the aircraft speed is below 30 knots, the helicopter will spin because there is no anti-torque to balance out the moving main rotor.

The only option was to do a "run-on" landing. That entailed maintaining airspeed, landing on the skids, and sliding down the runway, all while keeping the aircraft straight by increasing and decreasing the power. However, that also meant declaring an emergency when returning to the airfield. So I did. The fire trucks rushed to the flight line, as did the ambulance, and the whole world seemed to be watching. I had practiced for this crisis many times, so I made the perfect landing, getting cheers from the crowd. Aircraft, pilot, and gunner — all were safe and sound.

Later, at the officers' club, the story of how enemy fire had caused the dramatic landing grew along with the number of drinks. What had started as sporadic small-arms fire from the tree line became an entire company of enemies attacking us — depending on the number of beers. Then in came the maintenance officer, asking me to repeat the story of how I had almost been killed by this "devastating" enemy ambush and how my keen cat-like responses saved the aircraft and crew. The maintenance officer pulled an object from behind his back and showed me the handlebars that had been stuck in the pedals. He exclaimed, "The enemy must have been so hard up for bullets that they had to throw handlebars at you!"

Everyone laughed — everyone, I imagine, but the poor owner of the destroyed bike. It was probably the only way he could get rice or produce to market. But nobody cared about that.

If a mission meant going into a free-fire zone, we had free rein. On one such mission, there was a rustling of the bushes to the right of the aircraft about 100 yards ahead. I immediately turned my Loach and opened fire with the mini-gun, spraying 2000 rounds a minute. My gunner strafed the area with his .30-caliber machine gun. The bushes blew apart, and there lay two women with water pails. Neither my gunner nor I cared; we were in a free-fire zone, and it could have been an enemy ambush. Shoot first and stay alive — keep our pledge not to die in that damned place. Before we ended our tour, there were several more instances in which we did the same thing and got the same results.

I showed a particular disregard for the people and their struggle in other ways as well. I often took my new pilots and gunners on practice flights. I would demonstrate how to maneuver the aircraft, always keeping it moving in all directions. I would teach the gunner how to fire his M60 out of the side of the helicopter without falling out. I often used local fishermen's lobster traps as targets, again, not caring that some fisherman and his family would have nothing to eat, nor a way to make a living until he built new traps. But I did not care.

One of our routines, after a day of scouting, was to fly around the airfield to see if there was any enemy movement. At this last light mission, as we called it, we would look for anything new that might jeopardize the base.

I recall a specific last light mission during which my gunner and I spotted a significant number of fishing boats in the little lake near the base. The people in the boats appeared to be middle-aged men. The composition of the boats – only men – was unusual; typically there was a mix of men and woman. I decided to call the base. Command sent out a Huey and the gunships. The command ship with the local village chief said no one from the community that maintained the fishing area was out there at that time of the evening.

There appeared to be tarps or blankets in the boats, covering up something. I had my gunner spray a few rounds next to the boat to get a reaction. It worked, as several of the "fishermen" lifted the tarps and grabbed their AK47s to fire at us. The command to open fire was given. The gunships shot rockets with "nails." Once the rocket exploded 50 or 100 feet off the ground, it expelled hundreds of little nails. These nails strafed the area like raindrops hitting the water. It was devastating, killing many of the men in the boats and tearing the boats themselves apart. All the men in the boats now grabbed weapons from under the tarps or blankets and started firing back. Some of the men jumped into the water to hide under their boats. When I spotted one man jumping into the water, I moved next to the boat where he had jumped in; I slowed my aircraft to a hover, waiting for the little bastard to come up for air. When he did, I told my gunner to waste him. We laughed. Just another dead chink. They were going to kill us, so they got killed first.

That is what war had done to this young, naïve lieutenant. But I could get past it by merely "cowboying up!"

Maybe becoming a lawyer and helping people was my subconscious way of making amends. Learning to cowboy up almost destroyed me mentally. Could these acts of barbarism and brutality ever be justified?

On a more pleasant note, there was the time when my gunner and I wanted to get a North Vietnamese flag. On a scouting mission, we spotted a giant enemy flag on a large pole. However, we had heard that often the enemy would booby-trap the poles. My 19-year-old gunner and I came up with an ingenious plan. I would keep up my airspeed, and the gunner would reach out as we flew by and grab the flag.

However, there was a minor problem. As I got closer to the pole, it hit the skids and started to bend as my gunner reached for the flag. The pole then slid along the length of the skid. When it came to the end, it slammed up straight and the flag got chewed up by the tail rotor. Losing control of my tail rotor, I lowered the plane's nose to get up my speed and prevent the aircraft from spinning. But remember, the loss of a tail rotor requires an emergency run-on landing. Again, upon returning to base, I declared an emergency; as you may remember, without the tail rotor, the craft cannot hover. Once again I headed to the airfield and declared an emergency landing situation. And again, the fire trucks, ambulance, and everyone in the world came out to see the action. Ever the perfect pilot, again I pulled off a textbook run-on landing. The crowd cheered.

Again, at the officer's club, the drinks flowed and the stories were spun. Again, the scenario went from small-arms fire to a battalion attacking me. And once again, later in the evening, the maintenance officer asked me to explain how the enemy fire had caused the damage to the aircraft. I once again explained that my cat-like reflexes had prevented my plane, myself, and my gunner from falling into enemy hands. The officer, with a smile, reached into his pocket and pulled out a chewed-up North Vietnamese flag, saying, "The enemy must be hard up, this time, not even throwing bicycle parts at you — just their flag!" Everyone laughed. Another round, please!

# LAWYER TIMES

## YOU MAY PROCEED COUNSELOR

Once again, I found myself speeding up Highway 95/6 toward Tonopah to get to a hearing or trial on time. It was the same stretch of highway where I had found myself, as a young cowboy, lost in a white-out snowstorm. That was light years before. However, the desert morning remained the same as it was in my memories. It still had that crisp, clear stillness, and that coldest chill just after sunrise. The sagebrush still looked like silver crystals as the dew began to dry. It still spread its fresh, familiar fragrance, saturating the morning air. I am grateful that my memories of war did not blot out my memories of the early-morning sights, smells, and sounds of the desert.

After a two-hour, 110-mile drive, I scurried up the stairs of the romantic old courthouse in Tonopah just in time to hear the bailiff impressively shout: "Hear ye, hear ye, hear ye! All rise, the District Court of the State of Nevada is now in session."

Counselors sat at their tables. The court reporter's stenograph machine was full of paper; she was prepared to record every spoken word in the courtroom, even those no one thought she heard. The court clerk had all the evidence marked and ready to be examined when called for. The stern-faced jury members were ready to listen as attentively as they had promised during *voir dire* (questions directed to potential jurors by the judge and counsel before the jurors are selected). Then there were the quiet spectators in the gallery. All immediately stood.

Honorable William P. Beko, a mountain of a man, entered the solemn courtroom and authoritatively stated, "Good morning. Please be seated." Staring sternly directly at me, he clearly directed, "You may proceed, counselor."

I was ready. Still, it felt much like my early days as a cowboy. How many of these days in court would I face before I was comfortable and confident in achieving my goal of pursuing justice and fairness under the law and representing my clients to the best of my ability?

During preparation, each trial appeared to be "cut and dried" in the minds of both the plaintiff's attorney and the defendant's counsel. But then, the witnesses displayed nervousness, struggling and floundering on cross-examination. There were missed or overlooked details in the police report. Just one word or phrase could shed new light on the issues. Of course, that question you never expected to be asked, was asked. The entire case could change in a heartbeat.

These incredible, sad, unique and astonishing scenes were the guiding light and foundation that taught me to handle my trial work as I grew and learned. At the same time, I had to cope with the hidden secrets of my war past. How would that affect my ability to become a respected lawyer?

# LEAVING THE ARMY

After the experience of Vietnam, I had mixed feelings about remaining in the Army. A couple of events occurred that would tip the scale. I realized that the memories of the war were having an adverse impact on my life. I was unable to get some of them out of my mind.

Additionally, I had had a couple of conflicts with my commanders. The first had happened a few months before I left Vietnam, when a new leader took over our troop. He was a new major — cocky and headstrong, wanting us to know he was in charge. His first action was to order us to change the hunter/killer techniques we had spent months perfecting. I had survived over 10 months of combat flying using these methods, but I did not make any comments during the first briefing.

However, as we walked to the flight line, I told the gunship pilots that I was going to search an area the same way I always had. During the evening briefing, this green commander questioned my actions. I said that the techniques we had used were tried and true. It took some pushback from all of us, but finally he gave in and let us continue as usual. I, of course, got written up on the first officer efficiency report he presented to me. The write-up negatively affected my promotion potential, and I began to see the writing on the wall regarding my career in the Army.

After the run-in with the new commander, I asked the executive officer if I could be transferred, during my last two months, from combat flying to being a maintenance officer and test pilot. That wasn't my best move. As the maintenance officer, I almost killed myself a couple of times by test-flying the repaired aircraft. I realized I would rather take my chances in combat. However, the war was drawing to an end, and our unit was soon to be disbanded. The last month in the country, we merely loaded all of our equipment and returned to headquarters.

Turning in the equipment to headquarters was a nightmare! I had been in the unit for less than a year, but I believe that the unit itself had been there for several years. Throughout that time, the unit had scrounged up many parts and necessary items that were not on our official inventory books. These extra items created a real problem with accountability. As the number of non-authorized items grew, the commander told us to tag the items "found on post." We had a complete working Huey that wasn't in our official records, so we simply turned it over to headquarters, tagging it "found on post." Some of the smaller items we just threw in the ocean.

All our officers and men were finally loaded on the air transport, and we left Vietnam. I landed at Travis Air Force Base, the same base from which I had started. Not far away was Mather Air Force Base, where, much later, I would get a job with the National Guard as an instructor pilot during the day while I attended law school at night in Sacramento. After arriving at Travis, I got a cab, a bottle of Jack Daniels, and a case of beer, then headed to Reno, where my wife was waiting. I would get 30 days of leave time before I had to report to my next assignment, so was looking forward to spending time with my wife and seeing some of my friends. We would definitely go to the Pizza Oven, where I talked Linda into our first date.

When I arrived at the condo, what a joy it was to see her face. The tears flowed, and I relished her warm kiss and embrace. After so many days, weeks, and months dreaming of such a day, I had trouble realizing that it was, in fact, happening for real.

For dinner we went to Johnnie's Italian Restaurant — our favorite place during our courtship and where we'd had our last dinner before I went to Vietnam after my leave ended. It was the closest thing to the honeymoon we never got. We partied, saw friends, hung out at the Pizza Oven, or just spent time alone. I wouldn't talk about Vietnam, or even think about it, for that matter. We knew I had another two-year commitment in the Army, and while we talked a little about our alternatives, we didn't come up with any real plans.

All too quickly, the 30 days were almost over and we had to prepare for our next station. This time, we had furniture from the condo, so loaded a U-Haul and drove to Fort Rucker, Alabama so that I could complete my final two years of active duty as an instructor pilot. After arriving, we rented a great house and started making new friends. Some of the guys I had known in Vietnam were taking the same course, so we were like a real family. I worked during the day, while Linda kept the house and made great meals. We partied and had barbecues with the other couples.

The instructor pilot course was a challenge, but that was good because it meant I could not get drunk every night. I had to study and be fresh to fly in the clouds every day. The course involved hundreds of auto-rotation drills and operating only by looking at the instruments. I learned every symbol and mark on the charts; the words "Turn-Tune-Talk" are forever embedded in my mind.

Here is how it works. When you lift off, the control tower operator directs you to reach a specific altitude, then to remain on a particular heading or course. You stay on that heading and reach the assigned altitude. Then he gives you a new heading or course to turn to, and a new frequency to change to on your radio. You TURN to the new heading, you TUNE into the new frequency on the radio, and you TALK to the new controller. If you tried to speak before you turned, or if you tried to tune the radio to the new frequency before you turned, you would inevitably fly off course and fail.

After several weeks of training and testing, I finished the last check ride with flying colors and earned my instructor pilot's certificate. That meant I could wear the white circular plastic ornament under the lieutenant's bar on my hat—something I had longed for.

However, after I became an instructor pilot, I had another run-in with the commander. In basic terms, my sense of initiative caused me problems.

To help us teach instrument training, the Army had purchased a synthetic trainer made by Singer Manufacturing Co. This intelligent machine was a box-like contraption, which fit nicely in an air-conditioned hanger. The interior of the box looked exactly like the front seat of the Huey: all the instrument configurations, a pilot seat, and a co-pilot seat, with a jump seat for the instructor to sit between the two. It was set on four moving stilts and resembled a giant mosquito.

Best of all was that I could stop and play back what the pilot had just tried to perform. I could ask the student to take off, climb to 10,500 feet, turn the aircraft nose to a compass heading of 070°, tune the radio to a frequency of 122.6, and stay on that heading until I told him to maintain another compass heading. He would have to stay on course and not change the heading (i.e., the direction in which he was to fly). Then, on my screen (which the student couldn't see), I could monitor how he was doing. If the student got off course or tuned into the wrong frequency, I could stop the machine and play back the maneuver; he could then watch and see where he had gone wrong.

Our training syllabus provided for 10 hours in the trainer before we moved on to the real Huey. Though my students often didn't like it, I decided to make them do 20 hours on the trainer. Not only would I save the Army hundreds of dollars on aircraft flying costs, but my students would excel in their interim check rides with civilian instructors. The civilian instructors asked me what I was doing to achieve such success with my students. I told them what I had changed. They all decided to do the same.

The word got out. I was called to the carpet by the commander and reprimanded for not going through official channels to change the course outline. Once again, a write-up would affect my promotion potential. Finally came the straw that broke the camel's back — I was told that if I wanted to be promoted to captain, I would have to go back to a field artillery unit. There was a small unit on the base at Fort Rucker that I could have taken over, but if I was to stay in the Army, I wanted to fly.

After having achieved success in military high school and ROTC at the university, I was convinced that I would pursue the military life as a career. However, the effect of the Vietnam War and my experience with bad commanders quickly changed my mind.

With less than a year left on my active-duty commitment, I determined that it would be best if I requested an early release. With the help of my grandmother's political influence, our Nevada state senator, Paul Laxat, persuaded the military to release me, even though it had spent thousands of dollars teaching me to fly and to be an instrument flight instructor. I decided that I would re-join my uncle, not on a cattle ranch, but in his new business as a land developer, or on his property sales project at Kingston Canyon.

Back to Nevada my wife and I went. My uncle offered me a job working with him on his land development project, Kingston Canyon. I would have to learn about land sales and promotions, but it didn't sound too bad. My wife and I moved to Kingston and stayed in a trailer until our house was completed.

The plan was exciting. Carl wanted to develop the quaint little canyon into a miniature version of Aspen, Colorado. It was to be a small community nestled at the foot of the Toiyobe National Forest, just like Aspen was in the Rockies. The project looked promising. People were buying lots and building houses, and development of a little Kingston Village was underway, with a grocery store, salon, and office building. Carl built a fabulous stone-and-brick house right in the middle of the village.

The job was going well, but there was a fatal flaw. As I've mentioned, Carl was a heavy drinker, and as time went on the two of us got drunk every night. My attempts to keep the Vietnam memories repressed were not working; I would often dissolve into drunken, crying jags. My wife was distraught over these incidents. We started arguing, and when we both got drunk, we would even physically fight.

After less than a year, she announced that she might have to leave me and go back to the old job she had when I was in Vietnam. I could not bear the thought of being alone with my memories and without her, so I convinced her that we could take a new approach.

My first thought was to get back into the Army. I sent a request, but was told that because of my age, I would not be activated. I am sure they were also mad because I had pulled political strings to get out early. The second alternative was to return to Coaldale Junction and my grandmother, working at the bar, motel, café, or gas station. This option offered a way for me to sit back and evaluate future opportunities.

At Coaldale, I could keep my nose to the grindstone, which would help me put some of the post-war demons to rest. Good hard work led me to cut back on the booze and improve my relationship with my wife. Good hard work was the same self-treatment I'd used when I went through the flight instructor training program upon my return from Vietnam.

So there I was at Coaldale again, working at the bar, motel, café, and gas station, just as I had when I was 10 years old. This work would get me away from the nightly boozing with my uncle. I could now just work and think.

We moved into a little single-wide trailer out back. I decided to concentrate on working through the drinking issues and settling in until something better emerged. My wife and I were finally enjoying just being together and working. We also loved being with my grandmother. Jewell took a fancy to my wife and taught her everything she could about working the café and cleaning the motel rooms. After going to college and being in the Army, I would never have dreamed I'd end up back there — but there we were!

I worked a variety of shifts, both days and nights. Because it was family, 12-hour days were not uncommon. I didn't mind; what else was there to do if didn't want to drink booze all the time? We did go to Tonopah or Reno occasionally for a night or a couple of days off.

However, one complication arose. My mother, had lived in Las Vegas, and Tonopah, but returned to Coaldale to work, and it became apparent that my grandmother favored me over her. Jealousy was the result. Sometime later I determined that my mother had her heart set on taking over

Coaldale when my grandmother died and that she believed my appearance there would affect that plan. Consequently, there was some strain between us, especially when my mother got drunk. Linda and I tolerated it, but we were concerned about what we were going to do with our lives under these circumstances.

When my grandmother died in 1983, my mother and uncle challenged Elton, my step-grandfather, who, per my grandmother's will, would be taking over Coaldale. I stood by Elton and he prevailed. However, I no longer had a relationship with my mother or uncle. My mother died without wanting to meet and make amends with me.

# THE TRANSITION

One night I was tending bar at Coaldale Junction on the "graveyard" shift. In walked Judge William P. Beko. Not knowing I was at Coaldale, Bill was making one of his frequent stops for gas and a cup of coffee at 2 a.m.

Seeing me there, a university graduate and Army officer pumping gas and tending bar, Judge Beko remarked: "Young man, what in the hell are you doing here? Do you want to end up like the other drunks who spend their lives treading water and never going anywhere? Look at all your grade-school friends in Tonopah—most are deadbeats."

I confided in Bill about some of the dramatic events I had encountered in Vietnam, my experiences with some of the commanders, and how I had decided to get out of the Army. I explained how I had tried to work with my uncle only to fall back into the trap of booze. I described how after failing to rejoin the Army, I determined my only choice would be to return to Coaldale.

After listening to my story, Bill asked, "Didn't you take pre-law in college?" When I answered yes, Bill said that at Hastings Law School he'd had a roommate who was now dean of McGeorge School of Law at the University of the Pacific in Sacramento. Bill told me that if I did well on the law school entrance examination, he was sure he could convince his friend, Gordon Schaber, to let me enroll. Bill even promised that he would get my "cheap grandfather" to help pay and that I could also get tuition money from the GI Bill.

That's what got me into law school—a moment of pure luck followed by my ability to instantly and instinctively make the decision to act on it.

I set my sights on becoming a law student. I ordered a couple of books and started studying for the law school entrance exam. I inquired as to whether I might get a day job as an instructor pilot at the National Guard Medical Helicopter Unit at Mather Air Force Base in Sacramento. The guard commander informed me that if I could get into the Guard in Nevada, it would be easier to get transferred once I was accepted into law school. Therefore, I joined the National Guard in Las Vegas as a field artillery officer, taking a position as a first lieutenant and executive officer with a 155 self-propelled Howitzer company.

A little over a year later, I passed the law school entrance exam by a hair. I loaded up the U-Haul and headed to Sacramento with my wife, dog, and dreams.

I enrolled in a summer program at McGeorge. The first course was called "Agency," a pass/fail course. After that, I was admitted into the night school program. It was not necessarily what I wanted, but because I'd barely made the cut with the law school exam, that was what the dean offered me.

The Guard did not yet have an opening for a position as either a member or an instructor, so I took a day job at the law library. My wife got a job as a keypunch operator at a business in downtown Sacramento. With our two incomes, my GI Bill, and assistance from my grandfather, we would be okay.

The future looked bright. I was too busy to booze it. All it took was hard work, focus, and getting back into the study mode. I occasionally struggled with war memories, but for the most part, I was able to keep those thoughts deep within.

Law school was a new world of study. The professors did not care whether I passed or failed; they felt that it was the student's responsibility to learn the material. The first summer course was a struggle. It felt as though I had to know every aspect of every topic. Though my first course, the agency course, would not earn me a grade (it was pass/fail), I worked hard to get the "pass" result. I was also working hard to develop good study habits, and working at the library seemed to help.

I had mandatory classes, such as Contracts, Torts, Criminal Law, Remedies, and Real Property Law, from 6:30 to 9:30 p.m. on Mondays, Wednesdays, and Fridays for two semesters. However, even though I worked hard, my grade point average after the first year was insufficient for me to continue into the second year. It appeared that all was lost. However, after talking to the dean, I was able to petition the committee to be reinstated.

To this day I have no clear memory of what I said in that petition. All I remember is that I was straightforward and honest in representing my attempts to study properly. I informed them that I had not missed a single class. I do recall indicating that my Vietnam War issues were being resolved, and I knew that I could succeed. Apparently, whatever I said was enough for the board to approve my reinstatement; I could repeat my first-year core courses. The opportunity paid off — my score average on the first test was B- when C+ would have done the trick.

Over the next three years, I got that job with the Guard. I worked during the day and took core courses on Monday, Wednesday, and Friday nights. I also took electives, such as Wills and Trusts, and Uniform Commercial Code classes, on Tuesdays and Thursdays from 6:30 to 7:30 p.m. Each night, I would go to my makeshift office in the garage, sit at my old manual typewriter, and type all the notes from that evening's class. On the weekends, I'd study the material and prepare for the two tests at the end of the semester. These tests were all or nothing: get the grades, or you're out.

I had no life apart from attending classes, working for the Guard, and studying. However, I eventually made time for something else, because my wife and I were blessed with a little boy, Brian Elton, and a baby girl, Carrie Ann, during my law school years in Sacramento.

There is not much I can say about law school except that it was one of the most challenging projects I had ever attempted. The answer was clear: learn everything about every subject, and you might succeed.

One memorable experience involved the core course of Constitutional Law. The professor is now a U.S. Supreme Court Justice — the Honorable Anthony Kennedy. Justice Kennedy was impressive. I took lectures from him three days a week for a year. Justice Kennedy picked up the 400-page textbook only twice — once to double-check what page a particular case was on and the second time to double-check the spelling of a case. Other than that, the professor went through the entire book, discussing hundreds and hundreds of cases, from pure memory. Justice Kennedy said that if we could pass his course, we could pass any constitutional law course in the country, even at Harvard. His comment made me work especially hard in that class, and I got a B+.

Beko would have an even more dramatic impact on my life as a young lawyer. During my last year of law school, Beko hired me as his law clerk in Tonopah. I asked if three days a week would work. I thought I could use my grandfather's plane to fly back and forth to Sacramento. I had classes only on Mondays, Thursdays, and Fridays, so I could be at work Tuesday morning, fly out Thursday in time for the 6:30 p.m. class, then leave early Tuesday morning after the Monday night class. Judge Beko agreed.

Once again we loaded up and headed to Coaldale: wife, two kids, and more dreams. Though my grandmother had the apartment at Coaldale, she and Elton also had a home in Silver Peak, about 20 miles south of Coaldale. Elton's construction company office and the trucking yard were there, so Linda, the kids, and I offered to stay there while I worked in Tonopah and traveled back and forth to law school. I studied in the evenings and drove to Tonopah each workday to fly to Sacramento. There were a few bad-weather days when I had to drive over the Sierras, but all in all, the plan worked well. Not only did I get a leg up on how the legal system worked, I was also able to earn money doing it.

What a delightful day it was when my wife and I walked into the courthouse in Tonopah to see where I would work. The grand, classical building was constructed of large stones painted white. The tall doors were of hardwood, and the freshly mopped and waxed wood floors gleamed. The stairs led to the courtroom, district attorney's office, and law library, where I would establish my office. Up we walked, hearing the creaking of the steps and smelling the distinctive scent of the wood. We saw the large, stately bench where the judge sat when court was in session. It took our breath away, and my wife commented, "This is where you belong!" I agreed, and we laughed.

That was my last year, back and forth to Sacramento, spending one weekend a month with the Guard. And then there were the weeks I spent at various locations with the Guard in the summer. Travel from Silver Peak to Sacramento once a week, school, work, Guard, study — no time for booze.

Working for Beko was a remarkable experience. He was considered one of the finest judges in central Nevada (the cow counties). As a law clerk, and subsequently assistant district attorney, I had the opportunity to learn the trade first-hand from him. The draft research I presented to Beko had to be flawless, no excuses; he wanted the best answers. He even wanted research on each side of the case. My work for Beko turned out to be invaluable when I began studying for the state bar exam.

Graduation day finally arrived. The commencement ceremony was impressive, even including an orchestra. One of the top attorneys in California, F. Lee Bailey (who in 1995 would be co-counsel for the "trial of the century," the OJ Simpson murder case), was the commencement speaker. The dean placed the gorgeous royal lavender hoods on the backs of our doctoral robes. Tears of happiness and joy flowed.

What a celebration that evening with my wife, mother, stepfather, brother, and sister-in-law at our favorite restaurant, the Bank Building Steakhouse in Old Sacramento. And then there was the hangover experienced by all.

Another challenge had been accepted and completed, but one more major hurdle awaited: the state bar examination. Again, Bill Beko rose to the occasion, allowing me to take off a month to study. I could continue working for him after the exam while I awaited the results. He even talked Peter

Knight, the district attorney, into promising me a job as deputy district attorney in Tonopah upon my passing of the exam.

I put my full heart and soul into studying for the exam. We set up a large tent at Linda's mother's property near Virginia City. My former professor had a room upstairs at the University of Nevada Library. I would drive from the Virginia City foothills at 7:00 a.m. each morning so that I could be at the library when it opened at 8:00. I studied until 11:00, when I took a break. I played racquetball with a friend for about an hour each day, then ran two miles on the school track. I knew I needed to get in physical as well as mental shape to pass the state bar exam. I would continue studying and taking practice exams until about 5:00 p.m. I would catch a little dinner, then go to a B.A.R. exam refresher course from 6:30 to 8:00 p.m. Monday through Thursday. On Sundays, I even studied in a friend's law office. I took what felt like hundreds of practice exams and reviewed every course I had taken in law school. As when I learned to be a cowboy, I would not let up. Much like the time I had been bucked off my horse, each time I faced an obstacle, I got up, brushed off, and cowboyed up. As in Vietnam, I buckled up and headed to the combat zone day in and day out, without hesitation. I followed my grandmother's words: focus, stay on course, and don't let anything interfere with your goal.

At last! I passed, the license was sent out, and I was ready to become a practicing attorney would be able to make amends for all the bad things I had done during the war by helping people with their legal problems?

Once I was admitted to the Nevada State Bar as attorney number 00694, I was hired by Peter Knight, the district attorney of Nye County in Tonopah. I was also able to establish a private practice. In both roles, I appeared in Beko's court, which required a painstaking focus on detail. Any orders or pleadings I presented to Beko were almost always returned immediately, some even red-lined. Still, Bill's kindness, tutelage, and friendship were incomparable. A huge smile covers my face when I think about the very few times I was able to exceed Bill's expectations and receive a rare compliment. He was quick to criticize poor work or disconnected presentations, but he always praised a bright argument or an excellent brief.

I will always remember the time I repeatedly asked a witness the same question. Bill finally told me that if I asked the question one more time, he would hold me in contempt of court. But I had a plan. I knew I could not get the witness to answer my questions because it meant he would have to admit that he had committed the crime. So, during my closing argument, I told the jury that I was almost held in contempt of court due to my efforts to get him to answer truthfully. The jury found him guilty!

I was learning to be a prosecuting attorney. I was filing criminal complaints for almost every crime imaginable. I was aggressive, and with Beko staring down at me from the bench, I was also prepared. I realized right away that this profession was one I truly enjoyed.

# PRACTICE OF LAW BEGINS

I had an exhausting final year at law school, traveling and working. I had given all I had to pass the Nevada bar exam, and I was proud to hang the license on my wall. Now I was prepared to face the next hurdle — putting what I had learned into practice. As an old cowpoke would often say, it was time to "quit cutting bait and fish!"

I accepted the assistant district attorney job and joined Peter Knight in his private practice with Andy Demetras. I had known Peter for several years, meeting him through my grandmother. What I didn't know about Peter, or Pedro as we often called him, was that he struggled with alcoholism. The opportunity Peter gave me to start work right away was grand, but I soon discovered that Andy didn't want to work much. Andy had gotten divorced and lost his practice in Reno, so Peter took him in to help him. Andy left soon after I started and took over as district attorney in the historic mining town of Goldfield, 20 miles east toward Las Vegas.

I was excited to learn about the prosecution side of the law in my work as assistant district attorney. However, Peter was often drunk early in the day. As a result, I was thrown into the lion's den immediately, facing my first jury trial only two weeks after I had started. Peter didn't like doing jury trials, leaving me with sole control in the prosecutorial field even though I was as green as an Irish shamrock. Luckily, Judge Beko was presiding. For this first trial, Bill was very understanding and gave me latitude, something he would no longer do as I became more experienced. The trial went well, and I succeeded in convicting the accused. During my time as assistant district attorney in Tonopah, and a year later as assistant district attorney in Fallon, I may have lost only one or two prosecutions out of about 30 jury trials.

As I grew in the prosecutorial field, I developed a great relationship with the sheriff's office. Many of the officers remembered me going to elementary school there and teased me about how I had always been in trouble. Still, we worked well together. I was aided by my experience working with the old cowboys on the ranch, and the horses' asses of commanders in the Army. I befriended them; I even taught them classes on gathering and securing evidence. They would get mad when I had to tell them that they did not have enough evidence for me to charge a suspect with any crime. However, working together we were able to find a middle ground. The evidence was properly developed, and I could present the case with a winning conclusion.

It was not all win, win. I recall one of my first preliminary hearings in Beatty, located at the entrance of Death Valley, about 110 miles east of Tonopah, on the way to Las Vegas. It was a disaster. Judge Bill Sullivan was a newly elected justice of the peace, so we were both green. And, of course, the defense attorney from Las Vegas was a seasoned lawyer who later became my close friend and advocate. The case involved a defendant charged with stealing an ore car.

It was a beautiful antique, one taken from an abandoned mine owned by a local miner who had not found time to store it. The case was going well as we identified the item and described how the sheriff's office found it in the defendant's trailer. It seemed like a slam dunk! The defendant should easily have been bound over to the district court to stand trial. Yet, after I had rested my case, the defendant moved to dismiss because I had failed to present any testimony establishing the item stolen as exceeding $200 in value, which was necessary for a theft to be considered a felony. Judge Sullivan had no choice, and the case was dismissed. However, the defendant did plead to petty theft. He was fined and had to return the ore car. That was how I solidified all the skills I needed to prosecute a case — learning by mistake. Needless to say, I never again, during a preliminary hearing or trial, forgot to establish the value of items taken.

In rural Nevada, a justice of the peace did not have to be a lawyer. Most were very dedicated politicians who went to the Judicial College in Reno and learned the basics. I worked well with all of them. While in Tonopah, I dealt with Solan Terrell, a wonderful man who had been a justice of the peace in Tonopah Township for over 20 years. When I resigned as assistant district attorney in Fallon, I became the contract public defender for Nye, Esmeralda, Mineral, and Churchill Counties.

Because Tonopah was the county seat for Nye County, I handled most of the public defender work there. That meant dealing with Solan, with whom I enjoyed working. He was very fair; when I presented a compelling argument, he would not fail to dismiss the case, or rule that there was no probable cause to hold the defendant to stand trial.

Then there was the Fallon justice court, where I would deal with a very knowledgeable woman named Marilyn Gregg. Like many of the other justices of the peace, she became a very close friends of mine. She was an excellent justice of the peace, complementing me on my arguments or scolding me when I got carried away. I had many private talks with Marilyn about my days in law school and my work. She said that if I could do it, so could she. I believe my influence was the push she needed to apply and get accepted into law school. She later became a lawyer and retired from the city attorney's office in Sparks, Nevada.

Then there was Judge Trujillo of Hawthorne Township, one of my best allies. He knew that I had grown up at Coaldale and that I was willing to return to the desert lands of central Nevada, so he also became a close and trusted friend. He would always listen to what I had to say. If I had a strong argument as a defense attorney, he was strong and would not bind a defendant over to stand trial.

Finally, there was the senior justice of the peace in Goldfield, Esmeralda County. I recall a funny incident when I was a defense attorney, defending a DUI in Goldfield Township. Judge Joe Drew had been a justice of the peace for over 30 years. A great guy, but pretty set in his ways, and cranky. The arresting officer was called to testify about the arrest and his administration of the breathalyzer test. Andy Demetrius was prosecuting the misdemeanor case. On cross-examination, I asked the officer if the defendant had blown into the hose of the breathalyzer machine. The officer said yes, but that the accused had not blown hard enough to get a reading. I asked if the officer knew whether the hose was clogged. He said he had followed the standard checks of the instruction book, and that there had been nothing about checking whether the tube was plugged. Because the officer determined that my client had not blown hard enough to get a reading, my client was forced to take a blood test. The blood alcohol level from this test was about 1.2, which was .2 over the limit.

I objected to the results of the test because failure to check on whether the hose was clogged was an error. If the hose was, in fact, clogged, it should have been cleared. Therefore, no blood test would have been forced. As you can imagine, this was a rather unusual argument, but Judge Drew bought it and held that the blood test was inadmissible. The defendant was found not guilty.

Judge Drew was quite a character. He once put a defendant in jail for failing to pay his rent. I called the judge after the defendant called me. I reminded the judge that we could not imprison people for debt — debtor's prisons were one of the reasons the Pilgrims had left England. He reluctantly agreed, let out the defendant, and made the landlord sue him for the debt.

However, before I worked on my own as a public defender, I had worked very hard as the Nye County assistant district attorney under Peter Knight. In fact, I had done almost all the work because of Peter's drinking issues. I didn't mind because I was most likely getting three times the experience of those other young attorneys with whom I had taken the state bar exam.

Nye County is the largest county in the State of Nevada. The District Court was in Tonopah, where Judge Beko presided over felony or gross misdemeanor trials. There were three justice courts in Nye County that handled misdemeanor trials and preliminary hearings. Hearings were required so that the justice of the peace could determine whether probable cause existed to have the accused bound over to the district court to stand trial. There were justice courts in Tonopah, Beatty, and Pahrump. Beatty was 95 miles from Tonopah, while Pahrump was 170 miles away.

What all that meant was that when a crime was committed in the region covered by the individual justice court, either in Beatty or Pahrump, I would travel to one of them to prosecute the misdemeanors or to prosecute the preliminary hearing to have the accused bound over for trial in Tonopah. I spent hours and hours on the road.

This traveling was a good thing. I wasn't drinking as much, and my mind was filled with work and not memories of Vietnam. I was able to spend great weekends and evenings with my wife and two young children. We would travel to the mountains and chop down dead trees for firewood. We had picnics and other fun in the quiet desert. We would often go to Coaldale and visit my grandmother; we knew we could always expect a great free meal. My wife and I even became paramedics and drove an ambulance. It was either that or spend all our time in the bar, as there was nothing else to do in Tonopah. I transferred to the National Guard at Stead Air Force Base in Reno and became the executive officer of a medical helicopter detachment. Therefore, I would spend one weekend a month and two weeks in the summer with the Guard. I resigned after moving to Fallon.

A rememberable event occurred in Tonopah when Linda and I were called for an ambulance emergency. A man had been stabbed in the chest with a large knife. We managed to get him into the ambulance and off to Bishop, the nearest hospital, 108 miles to the west over Montgomery Pass, 14 miles from Coaldale. I was driving and Linda was caring for the injured man. Though she did everything possible, he died on the way to the hospital.

In a strange twist, I charged the man who had stabbed the victim with murder. He was ultimately convicted and received a sentence of life without the possibility of parole.

As time passed, all seemed to be going well, except Peter was getting more difficult to deal with. He would come in with a terrible hangover, and be mean as hell, or be a little drunk and sarcastic. One day, Pete went over the top. I had asked him about a task he had told me to do. He responded, "When I tell you to jump, all I want back from you is 'how high?'" Two weeks later, I informed him that John Hill, the district attorney in Fallon, had given me a job as an assistant district attorney. I was giving Peter my notice. I initially left with hard feelings, as Pete believed that I had let him down.

I would, however, repay Pete in spades! About four or five years later, Peter was stopped for a third DUI offense. If convicted, it would be a felony with mandatory prison time of one to six years. That would also mean he would most likely lose his right to practice law. Pete called me from the jail in Hawthorne. I immediately told him to say nothing to anyone and to refuse to take any tests. I drove to the jail in Hawthorne and talked to Pete. He explained that he had tied a good one on the night before and hadn't gotten to bed until about three. Then he had to drive from Gardnerville, 30 miles south of Reno, to Tonopah for court. Pete was now in private practice after completing his term as district attorney in Tonopah. Apparently, he was driving erratically near Mina and was pulled over. The officer smelled alcohol. Pete was smart enough to refuse to take any preliminary test, so he was booked on suspicion of third-time DUI.

I immediately went to work on a strategy. Peter explained the approximate number of drinks he had consumed the night before his arrest. I hired an expert to calculate what his blood level would have been when he went to bed. I then had the expert determine the standard burn-off rate and offer an opinion as to what the blood level would have been at 9:00 a.m., when Pete was stopped. The result was less than 1.0, the limit in those days. (Now 0.8 is the limit.)

Having a great rapport with the district attorney in Hawthorne and the justice of the peace in Mina, I offered to have my expert testify at the preliminary hearing in Mina. At the conclusion, we agreed that there could not be a conviction for a DUI because there were no blood level results and because the driving pattern was no different from that of someone who was tired. Pete pled to reckless driving, and was fined and released. That was over 30 years ago, and Peter Knight did not have a single drink of alcohol after that incident. As a matter of fact, he helped many friends through the steps of Alcoholics Anonymous. Pete and I became, and still are, the closest of friends.

So, goodbye Tonopah, hello Fallon. New home, new practice, and many adventures to come.

# STARTING A SOLO PRACTICE

When I made the decision to move the family and start anew in Fallon, I realized that I would be giving up the comfort of my support team in Tonopah. I had access to secretaries and research files. Pete did, however, give me permission to copy all the civil law form files he and Judge Beko had developed when they worked together in private practice and in the DA's office before Beko took the bench. Their data would be crucial to my personal practice.

John Hill was the recently elected district attorney in Fallon. He had been assistant DA for one term with Rod McCormick. John put me in charge of all the prosecutions, while he dealt with political matters such as advising the county commissions and planning committees. John and I worked well together and became close friends. Though I had worked for John only a year before starting my solo practice, we remained close friends and are still close to this day. After leaving the DA's office, John started his own practice. We often argued cases against each other, but always had a beer together afterward, no matter who won.

By the time I left the DA's office, I had handled a lot of jury trials and developed great rapport with the Churchill County sheriff and his officers. What an incredible coincidence — Dave Banovich was the sheriff. He had been with the Nevada Highway Patrol in Tonopah for years before moving to Fallon, and his youngest son Ray (known as Putt-Putt) and I had been best friends in grade school. We had a great time recalling our childhood days. Ray had also served in Vietnam, in a tank unit, and been injured. He recovered and became fire chief at the naval air station in Fallon.

When I left the prosecutor's role, I had a good grip on the criminal law aspect of my practice. As a defense attorney, I had to know both sides of any case, and I was soon appointed public defender for Churchill County. I also had a contract with the State of Nevada to handle Mineral (Hawthorne), Nye (Tonopah, Beatty, and Pahrump), and Esmeralda (Goldfield) counties.

After I resigned from the district attorney's office and left the courthouse, I was on my own. I rented a small office across the street from Rod McCormick, but I had to spend additional money for equipment and to find a loyal secretary. Rod would later go into partnership with a formidable attorney named Mike Macedon, who, in turn, would become the attorney for the City of Fallon. Eventually, I bought that little office building across from the courthouse, the one where I had initially rented office space from Rod.

Dealing with the legal problems in central Nevada required me to research just about every area of the law. I would handle everything from divorces, mining claim issues, real estate conflicts, adoptions, wills, and trusts to forming corporations and limited partnerships. Then there was also the public defender contract. I handled almost every crime we have on the books: embezzlement, arson, burglary, kidnaping, rape, home invasion, domestic violence, robbery, perjury, child endangerment, even murder.

It was a real challenge to handle public defender cases for more than 20 years. The biggest difficulty in managing the public defender contract was the daily contact with the bottom of the food chain clients. It is quite trying to handle fathers raping their children or druggies putting cigarettes out on a baby's bottom. It was difficult not to pre-judge them but to give them the best representation possible. Each time I faltered, I remembered a story told by my criminal law professor. He explained when he was first out of law school he was hired by the county public defenders' office. One of the first cases assigned to him allowed him to read the police report. The report explained that when police arrived at the scene, his client was seen standing over his wife's bloody body, with a knife in his hand. His wife was dead on the floor, apparently, the result of knife wounds. The accused had already been convicted twice of domestic violence against his wife. The professor said to himself that the defendant obviously did this one. When he interviewed his client, the client said he did not kill his wife. When he came home, another man was stabbing her on the floor, he wrestled with the man and got the knife way; they were rolling in blood over his dead wife. Just as he got the knife away, the real killer ran out the back, and the cops came in the front door and arrested him. His client had admitted beating her in the past, but he swore he did not kill her, even though she "needed it." The professor just went through the steps to put up a decent defense, not believing his client. About a week before trial, a man was caught at another home where he had stabbed a woman. He confessed to that murder as well as to the homicide of the professor's client's wife. He described the event to the cops just as his client had said it happened.

Each time I found myself pre-judging a client's statements, this story quickly brought me back to what I was supposed to do as a public defender. Give the accused all the rights the defendant has and make sure the Constitution is upheld in all matters of the arrest, collection of evidence, and interviews.

Several years before giving up public defender work, I realized that dealing with the bottom of the food chain was getting to me. One case, for example, came out of Eureka when I was appointed to one of several defendants charged with molesting an eight-year-old girl. I had the father; there was also the uncle, the cousin, and the brother who took advantage of this small child. She was isolated on a farm and had nowhere to go, no one to help her. The males were bullies, and the other women living there could do nothing to stop them. That was the first case after 20 years in practice in which I could hardly hold back the tears as I cross-examined the child at the preliminary hearing.

People often asked how I could deal with cases like that one. I could only answer that I must make sure the Constitution and laws were followed regarding the arrest and conviction. I may be able to exclude certain evidence, and the defendant could go free, even in such a hideous case as this one. The task was difficult, but my focus had to be on upholding the constitutional rights of the accused. I had to let the jury decide guilt or innocence and be sure that all the evidence presented was constitutionally sound.

I had to handle several cases involving grandparents molesting their granddaughters or boyfriends moving in with a woman and molesting her young daughters. I was even appointed to a couple of capital murder cases. I was the only attorney in central Nevada qualified to handle capital murder cases. One out of Hawthorne was difficult. My client had started a relationship with an older woman who had an 18-year-old daughter and a 14-year-old son. The woman soon got tired of her young boyfriend, telling him she did not need another child to raise. After a few weeks, he decided to get revenge, so he started "snorting" heroin off the bar, as described by the bartender at the preliminary hearing. The defendant then went to his ex-girlfriend's trailer, cut the phone lines, and snuck in the back door, where the young son was sleeping. He had a screwdriver and stabbed the boy in the chest more than 20 times, killing him instantly. He then quietly went into the living room where the daughter was sleeping on the couch and stole the keys to her car from her purse. He petted the family dog as he left and was caught about 120 miles away at a bar in Beatty where the cops found the truck, with the bloody screwdriver in the glove compartment. After the preliminary hearing, the prosecutor dropped the death penalty, and the defendant pled guilty to first-degree murder; he received life without the possibility of parole.

Another trying case was out of Pahrump. This mother and her boyfriend got stoned on meth and were disturbed by the crying baby. So, my client took the one-month-old child by the feet and slammed his head against the wall. At the trial, the expert testified that the blow to the head was not the cause of death, but the infant had internal bleeding and bled out. This case went to a full-week trial. My client was convicted. I had offered testimony regarding my client's ability to know right from wrong and the jury was convinced that the mother was the one who talked him into committing the terrible act. At the penalty stage, the jury recommended life with the possibility of parole after 20 years.

As I continued in my law practice, the sadness of handling these types of cases was again causing me to have difficulty in accepting people and my war days of disliking humanity were returning. I again became isolated, and I did not like to deal with people, even socially.

My wife then came to the rescue! She had taken a weekend leadership course with Rapport International. The participants stayed the weekend, Friday night until Sunday, at an isolated ranch near Las Vegas. The class took the students to emotional extremes. After she returned, she told me I must go, and she would not take no for an answer, so I went. The course completely changed me; I was able to view my fellow students in a different light. I saw that we all had the same feelings and emotions. The same cares and fears. I saw that we are all the same, regardless of race or "upbringing."

My wife and I got hooked on the leadership courses, completing Leadership II and Leadership III. All the classes were offered by Rapport. We were the only two married persons who had not divorced to become master leadership graduates. The view that all people have the same feelings and emotions helped me greatly in coping with the public defender cases, and other clients as well. I noticed that I became more caring.

We took the final course on teaching how one can focus and concentrate on what you want – not what you don't want. At the end of the course, we held classes in our home and taught the techniques to more than two hundred students. The finale was to have them successfully walk over hot coals in their bare feet, much like the famous Anthony Robins courses. It was a rewarding experience. We helped many people overcome their fears and problems. One student failed in his attempt to become a Navy Seal three times. After completing our course he wrote us and said that the focus we taught him worked; he became a Seal.

This new respect for humanity allowed me to cope with the difficult cases I was handed each week as a contract public defender.

However, the most rewarding gift from my wife turned out to be getting me into transcendental meditation. This meditation technique taught me that there was the life of reality, like splashing on the surface of the ocean, and then there was the ability to go deep down into the ocean and get in touch with nature and all it will give.

Meditating in the morning and the evening completely changed my life. When I was worried about a severe case or situation, I would complete my meditation program, and when I came out, I would have difficulty remembering what it was that bothered me.

We even completed an advanced meditation technique that included learning what is called yogic flying. This is a technique taught us to recite mantras resulting in yogic flying. Not actual flying but, without effort, we would hop forward several times getting the sensation of floating.

Again, after completing the meditation, anything that seemed to be a problem was no longer a concern. It is as if nature guides me and allows me to handle all situations.

The law practice start-up days were, however, filled with many changes as well. I distinctly remember what I had and did not have in the early days to produce complaints and file appeals. There were no multi-function copiers, just one sheet at a time. No fancy computer word processors, just typewriters with carbon paper for copies. Today, no one needs correction fluid. What a thrill it was when I bought a typewriter with a keypunch card for typing forms.

I then bought an IBM early-model computer from a client. I had to spend hours programming it with my secretary, Pamela Moore. She found it frustrating to use and would often fall back on the simple typewriter to do the work.

You'll get a kick learning about how we prepared all the pleadings and papers and exhibits for an appeal. When I was the appellant, we were required to file an opening brief and all the exhibits. There had to be six or seven copies. In the little hall, I built a long table on which we could stack six or seven piles of cover sheets and exhibits. On our standard copier, we could make only one copy at a time. Once everything was completed and stapled, electronic filing was unavailable. No, I had to drive to Carson City, 60 miles away, stand in line at the court clerk's office, and file the paper documents. Many a quick trip was made, usually on the deadline day when the brief had to be filed. If I did not get there before the office closed, I could be denied the appeal. Luckily, I never missed a deadline, but I must admit, my staff and I had many a midnight session to make sure I could file the paperwork on time. What a joy it was when I could afford a multi-page copy machine, then word processors, and finally electronic filing.

During my last few years of practice, I had a handy laptop computer that I could take into the courtroom. I could link into the database of the court clerk's office and view right on the screen every file and exhibit I needed. However, in the early days, boxes and boxes of pleadings and exhibits were hauled into the courtroom each day because no one could know in advance which document, exhibit, or pleading would be needed to show a witness or to file with the court.

What has not changed since my first day of practice is the need to stay focused and be well prepared for every case. If I "flaked out" just one time, the outcome of the case could change dramatically. In criminal cases, that one innocent defendant could be convicted of a crime he or she did not commit. In a civil case, the client could be exposed to a significant judgment that he or she shouldn't have had to pay.

Over the years, I gained respect from judges, as well as from other attorneys. Occasionally, attorneys from Reno or Las Vegas would come to Fallon, Tonopah, Goldfield, or Hawthorne and think they could take me on. What they soon learned was that I was always prepared and would prevail if they were not prepared. Some went back to their offices, claiming they had been "hometowned," but when they started talking to each other, the word got out: "Prepare well when going to the Cow Counties, because he does."

Over the years, I took pride in seeing and hearing the comments attesting to what a competent and capable attorney I had become. Judge Beko would have the jurors volunteer to fill out a questionnaire after the trial. The form was sent to the administrator of the Nevada Supreme Court. The judge and counsel would then be provided with a copy. I recall one jury questionnaire included a reference to my role as a defense attorney, indicating: "If I ever get in trouble with the law, I would hire that defense attorney!"

It was not long before I clearly understood why the *field* of law is entitled "the *practice* of law." From day one to the final days, there always appeared to be that one thing that was not known. Despite my having handled hundreds of divorce cases, I am aware that each instance has a little twist requiring a different approach to get a different result. Most attorneys (at least those who handle domestic relations) would agree that the emotional struggles involved in divorces and child custody are the most difficult. I often found it challenging to deal with the strain presented by both sides. Occasionally, they could not even agree on the time of day. I recall that, in one case, I bought the opponent a new flat-screen TV just to settle. After all, a half-day in court would cost my client five times the price of the TV.

I also had an interesting case dealing with a woman scorned. My client decided to take all her husband's clothes to the front lawn, drench them with gasoline, sip on a bottle of whiskey, and watch them burn. Another case involved a wife who was mad that her husband always came home drunk; when he returned drunk early one morning, she dove head first into the fireplace. She called the cops and my client was arrested. I did everything I could to get him off, explaining what she had done, but he was convicted of domestic violence. That, of course, meant he could no longer have any firearms in his home. At least now, to get a conviction on domestic violence there has to be more than just injuries and "he said/she said."

However, not all cases were full of hatred and vindictive conduct. One client and his wife had a beautiful young daughter. For the child's benefit, they settled their affairs by splitting everything equitably. They even worked out visitations so the girl could spend the summers on the ranch with her horse and her mother, then spend the school year with the father — a custodian at her school.

Another case was devastating to the children. This case involved the mother running to Texas and finding a court that gave her custody of her two boys. However, Texas did not have jurisdiction over the boys, who had always lived in Nevada, so my client got an order giving him custody. These conflicting orders meant that the boys could never go to Texas to visit their mother because, once there, she could have kept them in Texas forever. The boys were 14 and 16 at the time and didn't visit their mother again until they were 18.

A similar case involved a client who wanted to see his daughter, who had been taken to California by her mother. I advised my client not to go to California to see the girl until the court jurisdiction was determined and specific visitation rights were established. The father disregarded my advice. He went to California, had a physical altercation with his wife, and was arrested and jailed a year for battery.

Then there was the time when I had fun and injected a little humor into my closing remarks during a DUI trial. I had to explain to the jury members why they should not convict my client of driving under the influence. I explained:

> It is true; the testimony of the witnesses and my client verified the following events. The accused climbed into his car and headed up to "Sand Mountain," taking with him a large bottle of vodka and milk. He began drinking at the campfire with friends when a lady appeared, romantically inclined, and joined him. I know she never appeared in court because my client was too drunk to remember her

name after his encounter, but it is true that one of the witnesses did testify he saw this strange woman driving my client's car from the party, with him in the passenger's side. So he could not have been driving drunk back into town — the young lady was. Yes, I know that when the cops were called, my client was found, sleeping and stark naked in the front seat of his car, alone, a glass of vodka and milk that had soured beside him, and keys in the ignition. The handbrake of the car apparently had not been set correctly. Or when my client was "playing hide the weenie" with his newfound companion, he may have bumped the car into neutral, causing it to coast from the parking lot, crashing into the side of the apartment building, where the sheriff's deputies arrested him. And yes, I know that all the students leaving the apartment saw the spectacle, but no one saw my client driving drunk. Finally, I am aware that the law says there can be a conviction for drunk driving if one drunk is found behind the steering wheel and the keys are in the ignition. But where was he to put the keys? All he had on was a smile."

Verdict: NOT GUILTY.


In addition to the funny, sad, and unusual cases involving domestic relations, there were many tragedies. Two of my clients were murdered by their husbands. The fathers went to jail; the children grew up orphans.

The variety of civil and criminal cases a "Cow County" attorney took on may surprise or shock you. I, however, am a little biased because I considered the district judges in the Cow Counties to be more compassionate, fair, and uniform in their decisions than the judges in Las Vegas and Reno.

By the end of my law career, I could claim that I had worked on a jury trial in every district court in the State of Nevada. I will describe many experiences that were unique — and often sad — because of an unfortunate ruling by the judge or because of the shady conduct of opposing counsel.

# ART OF PERSUASION, PART ONE
# OPENING REMARKS

**Persuasion**

From Wikipedia, the free encyclopedia

*Persuasion*, a novel by Jane Austen. Illustrated by C. E. Brock
For Sir Walter Elliot, baronet, the hints of Mr. Shepherd, his agent, were quite unwelcome.

As my years of practicing law accrued, one truth always surfaced — the crux of the lawyer's trade is the art of persuasion.

In my early years as a prosecuting attorney, I worked diligently with the investigative officers, reviewing and evaluating the facts to create clear and precise evidence.

Let me explain how the art of persuasion comes into play. In a criminal proceeding for a felony (which usually carries a sentence of over a year in the state penitentiary), an arrest warrant is issued. Then the accused is arrested. To obtain the warrant, the prosecuting attorney prepares an affidavit to present to the justice of the peace, supporting the prosecutor's request for the issuance of an arrest warrant. The first stage of persuasion is in play. The judge must be satisfied, before he or she signs an arrest warrant, that probable cause exists that a crime has been committed and that the accused may have been the perpetrator. The deputy sheriff then serves the warrant on the accused and takes him into custody. On rare occasions, the defendant is told to report to the court at a particular date and time.

After the arrest, or if the accused voluntarily surrenders and appears in court, the court holds a bail hearing, usually within 48 hours, and an attorney is appointed to represent the accused if he cannot afford to hire an attorney. The attorney is ready to persuade the judge to set bail. Therein lies the second stage of persuasion. The judge then sets bail. The accused puts up cash or a bond and is released. If he cannot "make bail," the defendant is held until a preliminary hearing, typically 15 days after the arraignment.

At the preliminary hearing, the third stage of persuasion, the lawyers go to work using their skills and experience to "persuade" the judge to either bind the defendant over to stand trial, or to release him because of a lack of probable cause. The defense attorney tries to convince the court that there is no probable cause to hold the defendant for trial because the evidence presented by the prosecutor does not establish enough facts to constitute a crime. The prosecutor argues that there is sufficient probable cause to make the defendant stand trial. The defense attorney usually will not be given much in the form of discovery (evidence or reports compiled by the prosecutor or investigator), so his argument is based on the affidavit of the arrest warrant or the criminal complaint. The law in Nevada provides that, to bind the accused over, there needs to be only the slightest evidence establishing the fact that a crime could have been committed and that the accused could have been the one who committed it. However slight, I have often argued that there is no room for guessing or speculation, and that any conclusion must be based upon hard facts that can be lawfully proven. In my role as a defense attorney, I often challenged the use of evidence that was obtained in violation of the accused's constitutional rights. (unlawful search and seizure). I would drive home the argument that the conclusions reached by the testifying officer were based on speculation or guesswork, not on facts that could be proven. Thus go the first three stages of the art of persuasion!

Next, to challenge the evidence, various motions are filed, such as motions to suppress evidence on the grounds of unconstitutional search or seizure. The attorneys turn again to their skills of persuasion!

The next stage and, in my opinion, the most significant time during which to apply the art of persuasion is the presentation of opening remarks to the jury before any actual evidence is presented. The prosecutor is allowed to make an opening statement first, to tell the jury what he believes the evidence adduced will show. The defense attorney can give his opening remarks at the conclusion of the prosecutor's statement or wait until after the prosecutor has presented his evidence and before the defendant shows his defense against the allegations. As a defense attorney, I found that the best time to give the opening statement was determined by how strong or weak I believed the prosecutor's case was. When I was a public defender, the prosecutor had more "slam-dunk" cases because he could pick and choose which cases to take to trial and which to settle with a plea bargain. For strong cases, I would present my opening right after the prosecutor and before any evidence was presented, to give the jury a chance to see that there might be some doubt. Remember that to find an accused guilty in a criminal case, the verdict must be unanimous and "beyond a reasonable doubt."

One trick I would often play on the jury was to hold up the palm of my hand, showing only the palm, and ask the jury what they saw. "Is this a hand?" All would nod. Then I would turn my hand around and show the back side with the knuckles, saying, "No, both sides make up a whole hand. To determine if this is a hand, you ladies and gentlemen must see the entire hand. I represent to you that the prosecutor is showing just the one side; wait until you see both sides and examine the whole hand before you make up your mind as to what happened."

The opening statements mostly describe what both the prosecuting attorney and the defense attorney believe the evidence they present will show. Many an attorney must side step a bit after evidence is presented that does not match what she may have told the jury she would present. I have seen witnesses completely change their stories from what they had written in statements to the police. One time, the witness said, "The report was written to the cops because that is what they wanted to hear; what I am testifying to under oath is what happened!" Of course, the prosecutor fell out of her chair.

A great example was a case I had after I was in practice about 15 years. In 1993, I was retained to represent a young man charged with the death of his girlfriend. The trial was vigorously argued by both the prosecution and me. The prosecuting attorney was Kevin Pasquale, one of my former employees, who had left my practice and become a formidable district attorney of Churchill County.

It was a first-degree murder case, a tragedy involving the death of a 15-year-old girl. The prosecution claimed that my client, an 18-year-old underachiever, intentionally killed his girlfriend after running away with her from Redding, California. They were camping in a tent at Sand Mountain, east of Fallon, during a cold December. Tom Alward was a slender, good-looking young man. He was quiet and subdued. I felt that Tom was sincere in his explanation of the event; there were some inconsistencies, but I believed the trauma and complexity contributed to those contradictions. He had a rather sorry stare, which, coupled with his dark hair and black eyebrows, made me feel that he was either hiding something or was an introvert.

The sheriff's office conducted a four- or five-hour taped interview after he ran down the dirt road to the Austin Highway to flag down some help, and was taken to the sheriff's office. I was puzzled by the fact that, after the gun had gone off, killing his girlfriend, and after Tom had left the tent to get help, he zipped the tent door tightly shut. I considered it unusual but consistent with the actions of a frightened young man. That act, however, would later be a great benefit to the case.

The sheriff's office secured the area after the girl's body was removed. They also conducted a complete search of the grounds and the tent. This search was done without first seeking a search warrant — a fatal error!

Though Tom's story slightly changed a few times during the lengthy interview, I did not see a young man who would want to kill a young girl he claimed to love, especially because she cared for him even though he was not well liked in school. Tom's grandfather paid whatever I needed to defend him. We even hired an investigator to check out the girl's parents. The investigator determined that the girl had an abusive mother who had many men and some prescription drug issues. I used this to argue that the daughter had good cause to run away. The case taxed my abilities as a defense attorney. I filed motions to suppress evidence obtained at the scene without a warrant. During the interview, the sherriff's office gave Tom the chance to take a polygraph. I filed a motion to exclude this portion of the meeting, stating that whether or not a party chooses to take a polygraph is not admissible unless agreed to by the parties. I also challenged the prosecution's intent to show autopsy photos to the jury, as their prejudicial effect outweighed the probative or evidentiary value. I argued that the shocking effect would eliminate any benefit derived from viewing the dreadful pictures. I stated that the only reason for showing the photos was for the shocking effect of seeing this beautify young girl in the worst light. The dead girl could be identified using other pictures.

Before this trial, I had had a great relationship with and respect for the district judge, Mario Recanzone, but Kevin was his old law clerk, and I felt that Mario's denials of all my motions showed his prejudice toward Kevin.

I was able to hire some great experts, and the case was hard fought, but Mario's preference was obviously for the prosecution.

After that trial, I lost any respect I had for Mario, and I would bump him off all future cases until he retired.

Kevin was an attorney I admired, and I knew he would work as hard as I would in the preparation of his case. We had been going at each other for four or five years, and loved the challenge, but we always maintained respect for each other. Not once over the years did we deal with each other negatively. We both treated each case like Sherlock Holmes: "the game's afoot!"

Let me show you from the transcript:

In this particular case, Kevin's opening was classic:

> This case is about the life and death of Kristina Marie Baxter. This case is the oldest crime known to man. This case is about murder.
>
> I hope it is the only murder you are ever associated with, but while you are associated with this case, with this murder case, it will require your complete attention.

There is nothing complicated about murder. It is simple. Murder is unlawful and premeditated; it was thought out before it was accomplished.

In the days to come, you are going to hear volumes of evidence, Some of it may seem confusing. But the case itself, the tragic story that will unfold, is simply mathematics.

You start with two, you take away one, you are left with one. The one that's left is this young man on the end of the row here, David Thomas Alward.

The one taken away, the one that was shot, is 15-year-old Kristina Marie Baxter. Her nickname is Candy, and Candy was taken away on February 25, 1993, at Sand Mountain, east of Fallon, about two miles off the Austin Highway. She was taken away by a bullet that was fired into the left side of her neck, lower ear canal; it traveled 30 degrees back and 30 degrees to the right and exited at the top right side of her head.

The evidence will tell you that Candy was tragically taken away because she was murdered by the one who remains, David Thomas Alward.

In this case, both Candy Baxter and Thomas Alward gave us clues as to what happened on February 25, 1993, at Sand Mountain. The evidence Candy Baxter gives us is physical evidence, and the physical evidence that she gives us tells us that she was shot by someone other than herself.

The evidence is uncontradicted that the only person that it could have been was the defendant.

Start with two, take away one, you are left with one.

Now, the evidence that Tom Alward gives us is in the form of explanations. When you are down to one, you ask the one that remains to explain what happened to the other.

Mr. Alward tries, but he has to be careful, he has to avoid in his explanation pointing the finger of guilt at himself, and in doing that, he is never, never able to satisfactorily explain the physical evidence provided to us by Candy Baxter.
Each of his attempts to explain has resulted in more and more conflicting and contradictory statements.

If you tell the truth the first time you tell a story, you don't have to remember what you said, because that story is not going to change. It is always going to be the same. You don't have to try to remember what you said.

But this defendant, you will see, has been unable to tell the same story twice in a row. Each time he tells the story, it changes to reflect his perception of what the investigating officers, the interviewing officers, knew about the crime, and it has changed without any recollection on his part or any regard on his part for his preceding stories.

During this trial, you are going to have the opportunity to observe the defendant making these statements on videotape; watch him closely. He says whatever he has to say to wiggle out of tight situations.

When he is confronted with a tough question, a question he does not have a pat answer for, he deflects the question. He gives an inadequate explanation.
Mr. Alward claims that Candy Baxter took her own life, killed herself, and he will say that the only reason that he told so many false stories was because he didn't want the investigators to think that he had anything to do with Candy's death. Think about that for a minute, He didn't want the investigators to think he had anything to do with Candy's death. Therefore, he told false version after false version.

Doesn't your common sense tell you that people who haven't done anything wrong have nothing to lie about, nothing to hide? Is that conduct consistent with an innocent man acting innocent? Or is it more consistent with a guilty man doing his darndest to appear not guilty?

When you see the tape, observe his demeanor; is this how people act when they have lost someone who means everything to them, as Mr. Alward claimed Candy Baxter meant to him?

Witness after witness will testify that when this man knew we were looking, he carried on something terrible. But witness after witness will also testify that with all of that carrying on, with all of this crying for the sake of crying, they never saw a tear.

So you observe his demeanor, and you ask yourselves, is he suffering from grief, or is he simply acting the way he expects someone from grief to act? Acting grief without benefit of feeling the real emotion, because his blood runs cold.

Mr. Alward describes himself as not an innocent child but a machine full of anger, pain, hate, and resentment. That's how he describes himself, and those feelings, the pain, anger, hate, and resentment, are directed at whomever he perceives has crossed him, directed at everybody but himself, and Candy Baxter, at least until February 25, 1993, when Candy crossed the line, and when she did, she had to die, according to Mr. Alward's plan, a plan he had been formulating for days, weeks, months, maybe years before Candy was shot. Perfection is reflected in three major areas.

Ladies and gentlemen, as the evidence unfolds, look closely at the circumstances of Candy's death. Look closely at the real Tom Alward, a Tom Alward that will be revealed to you through his writings, and look closely at Tom Alward who is preoccupied with death, a Tom Alward with no love, no respect for anything or anyone but himself. A Tom Alward who when necessary professes his love for his victim, but whose actions in that regard speak much louder than his words.

He is so self-absorbed, he is so self-occupied, he is so preoccupied with denying his responsibility that he will go to any lengths to evade and fabricate, with the sole purpose of avoiding the simple but awful truth that on February 25, 1993, with deliberation, premeditation and with malice aforethought, he shot and killed his 15-year-old girlfriend, Kristina Marie Baxter.

Thank you.

Kevin's remarks are like a checklist of persuasion. Notice how he leads the jury to feel sorrow for 15-year-old Kristina Marie Baxter — her nickname is Candy. He explains the deadly gunshot wound. Then he asks the jury to look at the physical evidence and the defendant's demeanor in the videos to come. Slowly, Kevin paints a picture of the defendant as a calculating murderer, not a grief-stricken lover.

What must I do to counter these representations? See how I go in depth, almost three times the content, to challenge the simple remarks addressed by Kevin.

Here is my opening from the transcript:

> **Defense Counsel**:
>
> Ladies and gentlemen of the jury; the state has indicated to you what they think the evidence will be.
>
> This prosecution started by way of a request for a criminal complaint. There was an affidavit in support of the arrest warrant, and in the affidavit, there were four areas that they felt showed murder: first, the deceased had what appeared to be a grip mark on her left forearm or wrist area made by human hand.
>
> Secondly, the gun was in the deceased's left hand, yet the middle finger was behind the trigger, between the trigger and trigger guard.

Third, defendant kept changing his account of the occurrence.

And fourth, the deceased was right-handed, and it would have been difficult and awkward for a right-handed person to have self-inflicted the wound found on the deceased. As a result of that, the criminal complaint and a warrant was issued.

I ask you to observe any departures from that initial analysis, more particularly, if you are relying on experts, I ask you to make sure and pay particular attention to the source from whom the evaluations are made, what observations were or were not made, upon what facts do they reach their conclusions, and how reliable are the conclusions and the specificity based on their analysis.

I intend to tell you what I think the evidence will disclose. As the court told you, you are the ones to determine the facts as the evidence unfolds.

The state has explained the evidence in the light best showing his position, and I always do this, I ask you, what is this? Everybody normally says, "A hand." But I say, "No, we have half a hand. We have to see the whole hand."

So basically, what I am asking you here is my request that you do not quickly agree with what the state has indicated the evidence will show until you get the whole evidence.

Ladies and gentlemen, you have heard this story that the state has presented and what they think happened on the day on Sand Mountain.

Now, let's talk about Tom Alward's story of what happened, and what the evidence will show [about] these two different stories.

Tom Alward did not murder Kristina Baxter. The description and the evidence, in this case, will show you that when the gun went off and shot the deceased through the head, she was holding that — she was holding that gun to her head as if she was going to commit suicide. We will never know whether or not she was serious.

But what matters is that Tom Alward believed she was serious. He had been brought up around guns all his life, and it had been pounded into him that you never point a gun at yourself or anyone else.

When he saw Kristina with that gun to her head, he immediately — his immediate gut reaction was to get it away from her. He reached for her forearm to get the gun away from her, and somehow the gun went off; either Kristina fired or Tom's attempt to get it away caused it to go off.

Tom didn't kill Kristina. What happened was either suicide or a tragic accident caused by Kristina's ill-advised suicide joke.

Now, let's go back and talk about evidence in the case and what it will tell you about what happened that day. And remember, as we go through this evidence, we don't have to prove Tom's story to be true, in order to acquit him of murder; the prosecution has the burden to prove beyond a reasonable doubt that Tom's story is not true.

You will see that the evidence in this case simply cannot do this. It absolutely cannot disprove Tom's story.

First of all, the evidence will show you that Tom had absolutely no motive to murder Kristina and that he did have every reason not to murder her.

For example, all of the evidence in this case will show you that Tom loved Kristina.

The evidence will show you of their love, of the final resolve of Tom to be with her and to control and change so that he would be what they don't think he can be.

There is no evidence that Tom would have killed Candy in a rage of any kind. All of their friends and family and acquaintances at school were questioned about whether or not Tom showed signs of violent temper or history of fighting or resorting to violence.

There is no evidence to indicate that he would lose his temper against another person; in fact, all of the evidence shows exactly the opposite.

The many witnesses in the case, the writing, and the drawings describe Tom as outgoing, friendly, artistic. He tended to react to problems with poetry and drawings rather than physical violence.

You will see absolutely no evidence, in this case, to tell you that Tom is a type of person to use violence, and particularly not lethal violence.

And finally, Tom had no motive to murder Candy because he had many other alternatives. If they no longer wanted to be together, he didn't need to murder her. He could send her home, or dump her. There was absolutely no reason to murder her.

In contrast, as I told you, there is ample evidence to show you that Tom had compelling reasons not to kill Candy. The most important one, of course, is the fact that he was in love with her and planned to start a new life with her.

But in addition to these positive motives not to kill Candy, the evidence shows us that Tom had some very practical motives not to kill her; for example, everyone knew that Candy left home with Tom. Everyone would blame him if anything happened to her, and particularly, he would be sure to be caught if he murdered her in their tent.

Tom had a motive not to kill Candy, especially in the way she died because he was guaranteed to be blamed for her death just as he has been after all.

The state has no evidence sufficient to prove that Tom did have a motive to murder Candy. But on the other hand, there is ample evidence to show you that he had no motive.

The state also has no evidence to show that Tom is the one who shot Candy.

First, there are no witnesses to say that they saw Tom shoot her.

Secondly, there is no physical evidence to prove that Tom shot her.

Let's look for a moment at the physical evidence in the case and what it does and does not tell.

First of all, there are several pieces of physical evidence that tell us Tom's story is true.

Tom told us that he came into the tent, threw the gun down next to Candy, and turned around to fool with the radio. When he turned around again to face her, she was sitting down holding the gun to her head with the thumb on the trigger with a blank look on her face. He grabbed her arm to bring the gun down, and it went off.

Several things about the physical evidence support Tom's story. First, the physical evidence will show you that Candy was indeed sitting up when the gun discharged.

As you know by now, the bullet entered the left side of her neck, traveled through her head and exited out the right side of her head. Then the bullet went through the tent.

The evidence confirms her location, the direction she was looking, and the exit of the bullet from the tent.

The evidence shows that the bullet went through the tent quite high, and it would, and it could have only existed that high if she was indeed sitting up.

Experts will tell you that it would have been extremely awkward and unlikely, if not impossible, for Tom to have shot Candy at that angle while she was sitting up. If she were, in fact, holding the gun as described by Tom Alward, with her thumb on the trigger and held to her left side, it would more likely result in that bullet passage.

The evidence does not show that Tom was on top of her or holding her down in any way.

Secondly, autopsy reports show that Candy had bruises on her left forearm consistent with Tom's report that he grabbed her arm — forearm —to get the gun away from her head.

Third, the autopsy report shows that the bullet wounds — the bullet wound was consistent with what would happen if the wound was self-inflicted. In other words, nothing about the nature of Candy's wound disproves or even casts doubt on Tom's story that she was holding the gun.

In fact, our experts will testify that it is very unlikely that Tom would have shot Candy at that angle. It would have been very awkward if not impossible. If he wanted to shoot her, he would much more likely have shot her either straight on, in the temple, or in the mouth.

Fourth, the officer's observation when they first went up indicated that he saw blood on Candy's left fingers, a result that would more likely have occurred because of the circumstances of the shooting as described by Tom than any other view of the occurrence.

Once again, although there are a number of pieces of physical evidence that do not all support Tom's story, there are no pieces of evidence to prove his story wrong.

There is no evidence whatsoever to prove that Tom fired the gun. What evidence there is, is perfectly consistent with Tom's testimony that Candy was holding the gun.

In short, you will see absolutely no evidence of any sort in this case to prove to you beyond a reasonable doubt that Tom killed Kristina.

On the other hand, you will hear a great deal of evidence that will show you that Kristina was either really trying to commit suicide, or that she was trying to make Tom believe she would, or she was joking about it.

What would cause her to create the situation? First of all, you will see substantial evidence that Kristina Baxter was a troubled child who could very well have been — who could very well have been suicidal on the day of the death.

I want to summarize the evidence for you.

First of all, we have the very direct evidence of the poems she wrote on the day of her death.

Let's look at those for the moment. They will be admitted into evidence as an exhibit — that is, Police Number Two; I don't know what exhibit it will actually be when we get to it, but it will be a booklet that you will see in the pictures in the photographs that was, in fact, the one that Candy had and was using that day.

In that book, we find some of the following pages, and I am going in order. This is the first page. I will give you a few minutes if you can see it. I have blown them up quite heavily.

**The Court**:

Go on with your argument, Defense Counsel; I should say, your opening statement.

**Defense Counsel**:

Has everyone completed that one? And finally, in the booklet was a circular writing. That circular writing, I had to blow up 135 times to make it legible, but we find again what would create the situation. We have terms, and you are going to be hearing some language in the case, young people use this language nowadays, but you are going to find this evidence to be very critical about her state of mind on this day of her death.

Now, Tom told the police that he had read the poems earlier that day and that when he saw Kristina with the gun he remembered her writing them. She could very well have been serious.

Secondly, we have evidence showing the problem in the home. For example, we will see affidavits of Kristina's mother, Candy Baxter, and her stepfather, Burt Stewart, indicating the difficulties in the home.

There are specific incidences in February, September of '92, and according to the affidavits, you will see six and a half years of a terrible marriage situation. You will see from those affidavits an indication of using prescriptive drugs.

Thirdly, we will have the testimony of our expert psychiatrist. This expert has evaluated Kristina's writings, and the other evidence concerning Kristina's lack and has concluded that Kristina was very troubled and could easily have been suicidal.

To understand this testimony, we have to look at the evidence concerning Kristina's background and family life. Areas of the mother's marriage and divorces, the mother's problems with men, alcohol, drugs, her verbal abuse, and temperaments.

This evidence will clearly show you that Kristina had a very troubled home life, much more than her friends at school knew.

The psychiatrists will testify that Kristina was a perfectionist with a disorder called obsessive-compulsive disorder. She put on a very good front to most of the world and was honest about her feelings only to Tom.

Tom saw her problems. He told the expert psychiatrist that Kristina was obsessed with cleanliness. Tom's disclosures to the psychiatrist and collateral reports emphasize the fact that Kristina kept herself spic and span, meticulously neat. She would always have makeup on, was well-dressed, well-groomed. Yes, we will see from her journals clear, obsessional tendencies.

We will learn that obsessional phenomena are defensive maneuvers to reduce the anxiety of failure to perform the required act, resulting in increased anxieties.

Our experts will explain to you how Kristina would have been affected by the ten days away from home in a tent with no showers, inadequate food and shelter, in bitter winter conditions.

They will tell you that these conditions could easily have led a person [with] an obsessive disorder like Kristina to commit suicide.

The testimony will show that Candy had a conflict within herself between survival and unbearable stress, and she saw Tom as a way to rescue her.

We will not leave the items and interpretations only to psychiatrists. We have Diana Clayton, graphologist, who will...have another approach to evaluating the evidence.
Graphoanalysis is a scientific method of personality assessment based on research conducted over the last 70 years.

The writings taken to the scene by the runaways and the writings made at the scene and other places have been explored as to how they were written, little curlicues; the graphoanalyst will show a technique that will astound us all because, in looking at the way the writing is actually presented or written, we will see absolute corroboration or support of those clear findings of the psychiatrist, Dr. Rothman, and his assistant, Linda Kelly. The graphoanalyst will take us through a logical sequence as to the circumstances as [they] apply to Kristina, and show that Kristina may very well have committed suicide. The evidence cannot prove to you that she didn't, and it will very strongly support the possibility that she did.

However, we will show you that there is another alternative, that is, Kristina may have been kidding or threatening Tom to manipulate him. Candy was possibly setting Tom up to misinterpret her intentions so he would do what she wanted, seeking a solution out of fear that things might get worse.

The gun may have fired accidentally. There is quite a bit of evidence to support this theory as well.

There will be evidence indicating that Tom and Candy were into playing suicide games. They would try to come as close to death as possible without actually dying.

Tom threw the gun down beside Kristina when he returned to the tent.

She may have simply been playing another game; unfortunately, Tom took her seriously. Tom tried to get the gun away from her, and it went off accidentally.

And by the way, if Kristina were just grabbing the gun as a joke, it would explain why she used her left hand. She wasn't serious, so she didn't need to use her right hand. She just grabbed it with the nearest hand to get it up to her head before Tom turned around.

You will find that in volleyball she had the ability to do a left-handed slam, which also supports this contention.

Another possibility is that Kristina may have been trying to manipulate Tom by appearing to be ready to commit suicide.

Tom has indicated to the police about the fight he and Kristina had on the day she died. It may have at first blush looked like a simple argument over having an earring in his ear; yet to Kristina, it meant no job, no future plans, no dreams. One of the first passersby at the scene saw the pin in Tom's ear.

There is evidence, in this case, to show that Kristina enjoyed the power she had over Tom and that she believed she had considerable influence over him.

One of the documents that will be entered into evidence from her journal, and again, this is her writing, this is what she is telling us. As the state has indicated, she is going to tell us a lot. Again, I have made a couple of marks on that indicating what the evidence will show that she thought about herself, about her relationship with Tom.

On the day of her death, Kristina could well have been pretending to be ready to kill herself to manipulate Tom into taking off the earring or safety pin and getting a job.

Before I close, I want to talk to you about one more area of the testimony in this case.

The state wants you to believe that Tom Alward is guilty of murder because he acted guilty after the shooting.

The state tells us that Tom lied, and he tried to cover up what happened, and therefore, is guilty.

Our expert psychiatrist will testify about the meaning of Tom's behavior under the overwhelming stress created by the suicide of the woman he loved.

Remember, Tom told the police that when Kristina was shot he screamed, he picked her up, he held her; he kissed her, and he put her back down. He said he picked up the gun, planned to kill himself, too. When he couldn't find the bullets, he put the gun back in her left hand where it was and went to get help.

Would he have intentionally placed the middle finger behind the trigger if he was to set the scene? Our experts will tell you that Tom couldn't possibly think clearly after having just seen his love die before his eyes. He was experiencing intense stress just from watching her die, but Tom also knew right away that he was going to be blamed for Kristina's death.

Our expert psychiatrists will tell you that he came from a home where he was never supported. He was always criticized and blamed for failure. He was yelled at and humiliated and had an abusive and a controlling mother. He knew that everyone was surprised by his relationship with Kristina because she was the ideal girl, and he was an academic failure.

She was the good girl, and he was the bad boy. He knew that the teachers and Kristina's parents disapproved of him and thought he was a bad influence on Kristina.

Our psychologists will tell you that this background, and the fact that he was alone with Kristina when she died by a wound from the gun that he shot earlier that day, led Tom to believe that the police would assume the worst of him, just as everyone always had before.

The psychiatrists will tell you that he quite naturally was very defensive in trying to cover up just how close he was when Kristina died. He knew he would be blamed, and he was trying his best to prevent it.

But the police convinced Tom that he couldn't get away with lying.

I ask you to listen closely to the several excellent techniques the police used when you see the nearly five hours of interview to get to the truth.

The police convinced Tom that he had to tell the truth, and he did. Tom told them the real story of what happened that day Kristina held the gun to her head, either because she really wanted to commit suicide or because she was joking or trying to manipulate Tom. Tom tried to get the gun away, and the gun went off.

The real story of this case is as simple as that.

There is no compelling evidence, in this case, to disprove Tom's statements under very carefully planned interrogation. He told the truth, and that is what the prosecution must do to convince you of murder. Tom does not have to prove that his story is true. The prosecution has to prove to you beyond a reasonable doubt that Tom's story is false.

The state simply cannot do that in this case. There is absolutely no evidence to prove Tom guilty of murder, and there is more than enough evidence to create reasonable doubt.

When you have heard all the evidence from both sides in this case, if you follow the law and hold the state to its burden of proof beyond a reasonable doubt, you will be compelled to find my client innocent of the charge of murder.

Thank you very much.

It was my intent to show the other side of my hand. The evidence revealed that Kristina might have been suicidal and depressed because of her mother's conduct. The statements of my client in the interview would have been consistent with the physical evidence — such as the angle of the bullet.
So let the trial begin. The next area of persuasion will be our closing arguments.

# ART OF PERSUASION, PART 2
# CLOSING ARGUMENTS

The process of delivering closing arguments is identical in every criminal trial. All the evidence presented by the prosecutor is delivered to the jury. The evidence the defendant intended to present is also submitted to the jury. Then both the prosecutor and the defense "rest their case."

A closing argument is the time to argue or use your ability to persuade the jury to take your side of the story as the truth. The prosecutor always speaks or presents his or her closing remarks first. Then the defense counsel presents his or her argument, after which he or she faces the hardest part of the trial: letting the prosecutor make the last argument. The prosecutor gets the last word because she or he has the burden of proving guilt beyond a reasonable doubt.

After Kevin Pasquale and I finished our closing arguments in the Alward case and the jury was deliberating, Judge Reconzone gave Kevin and me a compliment for our closing remarks. Judge Reconzone noted: "Over the years as a lawyer, and even as a judge, I can say that I have not seen a harder battle fought in the courtroom than I saw with you two attorneys. Your closing remarks were presented precisely and covered your theories." Though I was pleased with his comment, I still felt disrespected by his conduct during the trial.

Let's take a look at some of Kevin's persuasion techniques in his closing arguments:

> **The court**: Mr. Pasquale, you may now make your closing argument.
>
> **Mr. Pasquale**: Thank you, your honor.
>
> Ladies and gentlemen of the jury, this is my opportunity to

sum up to you what I believe has been proven in this trial. But in a sense, that job has really already been done for me. Mr. Alward himself summed up this case — summed it up before it began, when he wrote this:

'Beauty roses laughing, smiling, bleeding roses, sobbing, sighing, torn apart love is lost, is it not love when it's not. Beauty roses running, flying, bleeding roses falling, dying; life blood crimson on the floor, can you tell me what's in store? Beauty roses free, and fine; bleeding roses, there are mine.

Bleeding roses torn apart, true love pouring from my heart; life blood crimson on the floor, look what you've… [remaining poem not legible in transcript]"

… I asked you to watch Mr. Alward's demeanor, watch it on the tape, videotape, watch it in court, watch his demeanor.

Now that you have had that opportunity, ask yourselves if his grief was real, or was he crying just for the sake of crying?

In that opening statement, I pointed out that you would hear testimony that he cried and he carried on when he knew people were watching, when he knew he had an audience.

You heard that testimony, and you heard witness after witness testify that even though he cried and carried on in front of the audience, carried on something awful, they never saw a tear. Not one witness testified that through all the commotion and crying they ever saw a tear, a tear of grief, a tear of sorrow, no tears, never.
Almost two weeks after that statement, here we are again, and during this trial, during that interviewing time, you have seen some grief, you have seen some real emotions right there in that witness stand, genuine grief, genuine emotion.

The grief of a mother as she identified the photograph of her dead 15-year-old daughter. That was grief. That was emotion.

You hear the emotions of Burt Stewart, an ex-stepparent.

You hear the emotions of Susan Baxter, a stepmom. You saw it. That's what real grief looks like, isn't it?

You and he saw that grief and emotion. You and he saw photographs, photographs of a dead girl, grisly photographs taken at an autopsy of a dead 15-year-old girl. We saw that. You saw it. He saw it. Those photographs would evoke emotions in the most hardened of hearts.

And you additionally have had the opportunity to observe Mr. Alward in court.

After I pointed out in my opening statement that he shed no tears – after witness after witness testified they saw no tears, then and only then did Mr. Alward ever show any emotion. He cried in court. Not right away, not when the pictures of a dead Kristina Baxter were exhibited. Gun in her hand, lying there. He didn't cry then.

Not when he saw the autopsy photographs. No tears.

But he caught on eventually. Eventually he got the message. Eventually, after hearing witness after witness that said no tears, he caught on, didn't he? He caught on in the middle of an audiotape that was barely discernible.

Ladies and gentlemen, didn't you recognize this as the same game described by Mr. Toffelmyer this morning? His former teacher. Someone who knew him. A game of manipulation.

Don't be fooled. Those were not tears for Kristina Baxter. Those were tears for David Thomas Alward.

Now the evidence that Kristina Baxter provided to us is far more tangible, more real than any of the inconsistencies in story and demeanor that were provided to us by Mr. Alward. Real evidence.

And we know from the muzzle imprint, keyword muzzle imprint, we know from the muzzle imprint around the wound in her neck that she was murdered. We know it wasn't suicide.

Now, as I foretold in my opening statement, you have now heard all the testimony, and I was right. There was some confusing, complicated kind of stuff, but the case remains simple. The case is not difficult. It is simple.

You start with two; you take away one; you are left with one. And if it's not suicide, it's murder.

Where do we start? How do we know it's not suicide?

The evidence Kristina left us, that's a good place to start. The combination of testimony that was provided to us by a board-certified forensic pathologist, Dr. Roger Ritzlin.

He conducted the autopsy. He identified the bruising around the wound and the neck. It was a muzzle imprint of the murder weapon. Put that testimony together with the expert criminalist, the firearms experts, David Atkinson from the state, Chuck Morton from the defense; they told you the same thing, didn't they? They told you this weapon, the weapon recovered from the left hand, middle finger behind the trigger of Kristina Baxter could not — and they didn't equivocate. They said could not under any circumstances have caused that muzzle imprint based on Dr. Ritzlin's testimony. Couldn't do it. This is just a

> gun. This isn't the gun that killed Kristina Baxter.
>
> The evidence is equally clear that Mr. Alward set up the scene to look like a suicide. He told you he did that himself, right? This is not hard stuff. He told you. He set it up to look like a suicide.
>
> The evidence supports that. The gun in the hand in the wrong position. It's merely a prop. The red notebook – lots of testimony about the red notebook. Well, the only thing we know about the red notebook is — both experts told us – we know it was moved after the shot. Both guys tell us that. So it's moved into position, isn't it? Conveniently placed by the lifeless body of Kristina Baxter.
>
> This alone is sufficient to prove murder…

Kevin went on to explain the various letters recovered from the tent. Representing that the letters did not say what Mr. Alward claimed they did, Mr. Paquale continued to emphasize that all Alward's statements were mere props, supporting a suicide scam. He specifically stressed that by saying:

> … All that suicide mumbo-jumbo came from one source, uncorroborated by anyone, and that one source is the only source. The only source that has a need, a reason for there to have been a suicide here. Mr. Alward ….

> ... the crime scene at Sand Mountain is a stage. Mr. Alward was a director, set his props out. The gun, the notebook. The body of a 15-year-old girl. Her death is a personal statement and Mr. Alward plays on the philosophy of life, which is really a philosophy of death. An expression of his hate and contempt for those around him.
>
> And finally his lies, lies, evasions, and deceptions. The master manipulator pulling the wool over the eyes of those hick cops in rural Nevada who tried to interview him, hick cops in Fallon, Nevada, who never encountered the likes of Tom Alward before.
>
> The defendant underestimated the rest of the world. A world that still values truth. Still values justice, still feels compassion and concern for a stranger, a 15-year-old stranger named Kristina Baxter, born April 12, 1977, who never saw her 16th birthday, won't graduate from high school. Won't play basketball again, won't go camping again.

Mr. Pasquale ended by again reading the hateful language of the poem written by Tom and taken from the tent. Ending with:

> > ... We live in a world which values truth, what is right. A world where justice is done.
> >
> > What does Mr. Alward's world value? Falsehood, hate, and death, and that is your choice. You alone will decide

> the legacy of Kristina Baxter. A 15-year-old who came to a tragic, untimely end in our county.
>
> What is to be done is in your hands. Thank you.

As I started my closing remarks, as usual, I reminded the jury that this would be the last time I would speak, and Mr. Pasquale would be able to have an ending closing because he had the burden to prove guilt.

> **The Court**: Defense Counsel, you may proceed with your closing arguments.
>
> **Defense Counsel**: Thank you, your honor.
>
> ... In this case, I started by telling you that the state told you what they thought had happened. The state has now indicated what they thought the evidence was.
>
> I also asked you not to decide the case before you saw the entire hand. I indicated to you that the statements (of counsel) are not evidence, but merely what we think the evidence shows.
>
> But I didn't depart from my opening remarks as suggested by the state. I opened by saying the state initiated this prosecution by indicating in an affidavit that there was a basis for murder because the deceased had what appeared to be grip marks on her left forearm made by a human hand. The gun was in the deceased's

left hand, yet the middle finger was behind the trigger, between the trigger guard. The defendant kept changing his account of the occurrence. The deceased was right-handed. And it would have been awkward or difficult for a right-handed person to have self-inflicted the wound.

But I also asked you to examine the testimony and to observe what departures, if any, the state made from its initial analysis.

It appears that they have come up with a new theory that it was a nine-millimeter gun.

Let's review some of the salient facts that may support their theory.

They did in fact call Candy Lynn Stewart. She told us of a good girl who had no reason to run away from home. She told us of a broken marriage. But Kristina was not concerned except for the financial impact. She told us that she offered birth control to Kristina. She indicated that she had a good daughter who ran away. She indicated that she had occasionally smoked pot at home. But there appears to be no evidence in her testimony that points to murder.

Officer Bogdanowitcz. He disclosed that upon arrival at the scene he observed the accused sitting off to the side of the road. He seemed upset, distraught. The officer was the first to see the deceased, and he noticed blood on her left hand and blood on her shoulder. No life signs. Again, no indication of murder.

Office Wood. He told us of a five- to five-and-a-half-hour interview with two seasoned officers using well-trained, established interrogation techniques. What type of inducement to tell the truth. You heard the tape. I counted 52 separate statements concerning inducement to tell the truth. Again, that testimony does not indicate murder. It may indicate guilt about not telling the truth at first.

The next one, Joseph Kemper, related what Tom told us about the incident, Tom's difficulties, and the cold. No indication of murder.

Michael Lloyd Davis related what Tom told about the incident; related that Tom waited outside for what he thought was 45 minutes to an hour; indicated that when Tom came to the window, he appeared to be crying; indicated what a scared boy would say under the circumstances. No indication of murder.

Brian Jorgensen, the highway patrolman. This officer takes Tom into his confidence. He gives him a warm car. Tom breaks down. His secret mic captures the true Tom. Is Tom scared? Is he emotional? Didn't you hear the tape, didn't you hear Tom? You can. It's in evidence, that was Tom.

That's the first one that showed some compassion for Tom.

Jim Stewart. He testified, described what he noticed: the blood on the deceased's fingers: described that he noticed what appeared to be human grip marks on the left wrist. And, of course, he told us about the mountain of evidence found at the scene.

But he told us one other thing. He also told us that two weeks before trial, he, the district attorney, and Dr. Ritzlin met and discussed suspicions of another gun as the object causing the death. But again in his testimony no indication of murder.

Next we have Dr. Ritzlin. We see clearly his findings in his initial autopsy report: no notations of bruising or muzzle impressions; yet we also heard him tell us about a conference with the D.A. and the investigator about bruising and muzzle imprints. But again, no indication of murder.

David Atkinson told us that if you believed Dr. Ritzlin's newly discovered bruising or muzzle impressions were true, he could not imagine a revolver having made the wound. But again, no indication of murder.

Do you recall in my opening that the first thing I told you was that you had heard the state's story of what they think happened that day on Sand Mountain? Well, the witnesses and the documents the state relied on to establish murder have been presented. But where is the evidence of murder?

Tom Alward did not murder Kristina Baxter. Tom's description and the evidence in the case show you that when the gun went off and shot the deceased in the head, she was holding the gun in her hand as if she were going to commit suicide. We will never know whether or not she was serious.

I also noted that what matters is that Tom believed she was serious. He had been brought up around guns all his life, and it had been pounded into him never to point a gun at yourself or another. So, when he saw Kristina with the gun, that gun to her head, his immediate gut reaction was to get it away from her, but somehow the gun went off. Either Kristina fired it or Tom's attempt to get it away from her caused it to go off.

Where is the evidence to prove beyond a reasonable doubt that this is not what happened?

Tom didn't kill Kristina Baxter. What happened was either her attempted suicide or a tragic accident caused by Kristina's ill-advised suicide joke or attempt...

... All the evidence in this case shows you that Tom loved Kristina. The evidence shows Tom and Kristina's love, and their final resolve to be together. The evidence from Tom's own writings shows that he loved Kristina, and from her writings that she believed he loved her and that she was good for him.

Why would Tom murder a woman he loved?

There is absolutely no evidence in this case that Tom lured Kristina away from her home so that he could murder her. All of the evidence we have, including letters from Kristina to her mother and friends, tells us that they left home to be together. They wanted to start a new life together, away from what they viewed as unsolvable problems with the parents or a life they didn't want.

The letter that was to be sent from Tom to his mother and father was intended to scare them into not trying to find the two young lovers. But more importantly, it indicated a plan to start a new life with her, where he could be a success.

There is no evidence that he planned to kill her.

There is no evidence that Tom would have killed Candy in a rage of any kind.

There is no evidence that Tom showed any signs of violent temper or history of fighting or resorting to violence, especially against another person.

There is absolutely no evidence in this case to tell you that Tom is the type of person to use violence against another person, particularly lethal violence.

And, finally, Tom had no motive to murder Candy because he had many

— as I said in my opening — he had many alternatives. He didn't have to murder her. He could have sent her home. He could have just dumped her, as they say.

There is absolutely no reason to murder her if they were going to break up.

In contrast, as I told you, there is ample evidence that shows you that Tom had compelling reasons not to kill Candy. The most important, of course, is the fact that he was in love with her and planned to start a new life with her….

… There are several pieces of evidence that tell us that Tom's story is true. … the evidence is absolutely clear that she was sitting because we have these three angles. We have where it was in the tent. She was sitting. That's concrete, hard evidence.

Chuck Morton stated the situation the best when he testified.

… The fact that there is an autopsy report that does not mention bruises, and that does not mention the configuration of an imprint, which is a critical piece of information, raises some questions about the assessment that came after the autopsy and was given at the trial after the discussion with the district attorney….

… To make a determination that there was, in fact, bruising and muzzle imprints, there would need to have been a clean wound and photograph to show what they are talking about. Or a least a description in the report, because it is not reflected in what I am saying here about the photograph. The angle of the shot would create smoke or sooting, not a muzzle imprint.

Mr. Rick — Dr. Rayn and Mr. Morton have one common thread in the findings — if findings are not documented, there is no way to substantiate the findings.

I suggest that false conclusions are not facts that can be used to convict.

…

… the state's case is not supported by evidence. There is no element establishing murder. There is no evidence that would indicate that David Thomas Alward murdered the girl he loved, Kristina Baxter. No motive, no intent to kill. No premeditation. No guilt.

Don't you have reasonable doubt about what really happened at Sand Mountain?

Thank you very much.

The matter was then turned over to the jury for deliberation. My recollection is that the jury spent several hours, maybe over a two-day period, and came back with a verdict of guilty of second-degree murder.

I appealed the verdict to the Nevada Supreme Court, and the case was reversed on the basis that the state had used evidence taken from the tent that violated the defendant's rights with respect to search and seizure. The tent was surrounded by the sheriff's "Do Not Enter" tape and officers securing the scene. No emergency circumstances would have prevented them from getting a search warrant. The officers removed the body and zipped the tent. They then returned to search and gather evidence, but did not have a warrant.

After winning the appeal, the matter was remanded for a new trial. Tom had spent three years in prison at that time, so the state agreed to let him plead to manslaughter with time served.

Each and every criminal or even civil trial forced me to develop skills in persuasion. The stamina I learned on the ranch and in dealing with combat kept me focused and ready to face any arguments from opposing counsel.

Being a trial attorney was an exciting job for me over a span of more than 35 years. The variety of cases, both civil and criminal, greatly helped me overcome the stress and memories of my combat experiences. I believe I provided a needed service to my Cow County folks.

# LAW PRACTICE ENDS IN A WHIRLWIND

After over 25 years dealing with public defender clients, I was offered the opportunity to join a company as in-house counsel. The two- to four-hour daily drives had become more and more difficult. Although I'd been thinking about making a change, an unusual occurrence with one of my public defender clients made up my mind. I was reviewing the complaint, a charge of the sale of a controlled substance, and I recognized the name. However, the defendant was too young to be the person I was thinking of, so I asked, "Didn't I represent your father on the same charge a few years back?"

"Yes," he responded. "Oh — and my grandfather too!"

I said to myself, "I have to get out of here; dealing with this is burning me out."

A few weeks later, some former clients appeared in Hawthorne on one of my law and motions days, so named because this was the day of the week when the district court handled arraignments to set a trial, pleas, and sentencing. I recognized them sitting in the hall and said, "What are you doing here? I seem to remember forming a couple of corporations and handling some mining questions for you four or five years ago?"

The CEO said, "We have a new project, and we would like to hire you to evaluate it. We've filed a lot of mining claims south of Las Vegas and have a business plan we'd like you to look over. I want to put you on a retainer — five thousand a month."

I said, "That sounds great! Give me the plan and I'll review it and give you my opinion." They invited me to lunch and gave me the plan.

The idea was quite simple — the mining claims that were "staked" would be divided (usually 20 acres) into smaller areas, i.e., five acres or 10 acres to be sold to interested buyers. A deed would be written to describe the acres that the investor would be buying. That deed would transfer ownership of that portion of the mining claim to the buyer, and would be recorded with the county and the Bureau of Land Management [BLM]. The purchase agreement was to include the earning of interest on their investment (around 10 percent) until a mining plan was approved and the company got into production. The interest payments would then come out of the mining operation.

Thus started a new adventure. Goodbye public defender and private practice. I did, however, hire an old classmate to maintain my private practice as a backup.

To my dismay, after I had worked on the project for over two years, Forbes magazine wrote an article about the project out of Las Vegas, and for the first time, I learned that the CEO had been convicted in Arizona of violating Securities and Exchange Commission regulations by selling securities without a license. The government would consider the purchase agreement, coupled with the deed, to be a financial arrangement involving a pledge of collateral. As I later learned, the note was not secured by any real value. Because the claims were not being mined, the note was unsecured and was therefore considered a security requiring the acquisition of a license before sale. Neither the company nor the board members had received such a license.

After the Forbes article, I also learned that the CEO had been involved in a scam out of Mexico in which he had aided in the sale of interests in condos in what had turned out to be a Ponzi scheme.

In addition, I learned that the CEO had used a sales team to sell the Mexico properties. What I didn't know was that the same group had been brought to Las Vegas to sell the mining claims and develop a mining operation.

I also discovered that a fraud was being committed in the taking of the mineral samples from each claim. I learned that the vice president was taking samples from only the highest-concentration area and claiming they were from each claim — not from each individual claim, as represented. I went through the ceiling, as did the CEO, who claimed he knew nothing about the activity. The CEO's son took over taking samples and marked with GPS coordinates each area where the samples had been taken. The vice president was then removed from the board of directors. However, I would later learn that because the vice president had been fired, he went to the feds and claimed the CEO was the king of "Ponzi." The feds eventually filed a criminal complaint against the CEO and his son as a result of the vice president's disclosures.

When I first became in-house counsel, I developed what I thought was a legitimate contract for the purchase of individual mining claims that would provide a return on their purchase in the form of monthly payments. I envisioned the CEO pursuing a mining operation that would produce income to pay the monthly contract payment. He did not diligently pursue the mining operation, but wanted to claim that the minerals on the claims were valuable by adding "Willard Water." Willard Water was an additive that was purported to enhance the minerals in the soil. It had been developed by a pharmacist out of the Midwest. However, I was never shown any proof that this additive would enhance the minerals in the soil to be mined.

I didn't find out until the company tried to get a mining plan approved that the mineral discovery was not an actual discovery. There were no different minerals to be considered as a discovery, so the

Bureau of Land Management (BLM) rejected the plan. The rejection of the operating mining plan was initially a surprise to me because the CEO had gotten a licensed mining appraiser to appraise the mining claims, establishing over $50 million in value if mined. But again, the BLM didn't buy it and would not grant a mining plan until the BLM did its own evaluation, for which the mining company had to advance $300,000.

Even after the BLM rejection, I learned that the CEO had kept selling mining claims, collecting money, and using some of the money to give the purchasers the monthly interest payments promised for their investment. Again, that conduct, as I soon learned after the filing of a civil complaint by the SEC, amounted to selling securities without a license.

I was personally named in the SEC civil complaint because I had been elected to the board when the vice president was removed. For three years I would fight my being named in the civil action for securities violations.

Within two years after the filing of the criminal complaint, the company was dissolved, and the CEO and his son took a plea bargain on the criminal charges.

After this fiasco, though I continued fighting the SEC, I returned to Fallon and reactivated my law practice. This reactivation occurred at the time when the issues relating to sub-prime mortgages started coming to light. I decided I would embark on what would become a three-year quest to go after the banks. I formulated a complaint claiming that the banking industry had developed a "predatory lending scheme."

I often questioned my abilities as a trial lawyer when dealing with many of the same attorneys and judges in the Cow Counties of central Nevada. Nevertheless, during these last three years of practice, when I decided to take on the banks and title companies, I knew I would be going against the best lawyers in the country — those who represented the Big Banks.

I had to fight hundreds of motions to dismiss, and I did so in every department in the Reno District Court, some of the Cow Counties, and the federal court for the Northern Division of Nevada.

My art of persuasion shone in comparison to that of many out-of-state lawyers from New York, Washington D.C., Chicago, and Los Angeles, and even compared to those from the large law firms in Las Vegas. It wasn't long before the judges who hadn't seen me before, especially the federal judges, began to recognize that this Cow County bumpkin lawyer had considerably more experience at presenting arguments and persuasion than the "city slickers" did. The judges didn't know that the skills I had developed as a cowboy and warrior helped me overcome challenges.

The test was unlike any I had faced before. How does one argue when his client signed a note to buy a home and then stops paying?

I started working with two well-respected attorneys whose office was in Reno. Bob Hagger and his partner, Triva Hern, had developed a complaint involving a "predatory lending scheme." They were pursuing their claims from a class-action approach. This meant that they were placing all their plaintiffs on one complaint and treating the harm caused by the banks as being against a particular class of people.

I, on the other hand, believed that each homeowner had a separate, independent claim, so I developed my complaint with different causes of actions being brought by each individual.

Taking on the challenge and putting my skills to the test reminded me of the moment, as a cowboy, when I knew I was a good horseman. There was no fear, no intimidation, just pure confidence.

There were hearings in court during which I stood alone at the plaintiff's table while six or seven attorneys at the defense table argued for the banks or other defendants, each taking a shot at me.

I became an advocate for exposing the terrible practice of predatory lending. The complaints I developed were exhaustive, but I knew I had to get the court's attention and educate the judges about a relatively new way of thinking. I needed to convince them that the complaint was not just about signing a note and not paying. It was about being lured into a deal that was apparently doomed to fail from the outset.

There were only a half-dozen attorneys in northern Nevada who decided to take on the challenge of dealing with the tactics of the big firms. Their primary tactic was to bury us plaintiff's attorneys in piles of paperwork in the form of motions, depositions, and requests for removal from state court to federal court.

In my efforts to "educate" the court, I included the following language:

> "The best definition that I have found is as follows:
>
>> Predatory lending as a syndrome of abusive loan terms or practices that involve one or more of the following five problems:
>>
>> (1) loans structured to result in severely disproportionate net harm to borrowers,
>>
>> (2) harmful rent-seeking,

> (3) loans involving fraud or deceptive practices,
>
> (4) other forms of lack of transparency in loans that are not actionable as fraud, and
>
> (5) loans that require borrowers to waive meaningful legal redress…"

I had to get the courts to comprehend the ways in which consumers were lured into loans that ultimately failed when the standard payment amount kicked in. The real damage, as we have now recognized, is that this system of giving anyone a loan was also a fraud on the part of the securitied trust putting up the endless source of funds.

I laid out an explanation as to how the banks were getting the money and loaning it anyone who had a pulse. The idea behind presenting this foundational information was that I believed the judges had never seen or heard about the conduct of the various lenders.

My primary attack was claiming that those entities that were commencing foreclosures were not real parties in interest to the transaction. These companies were hired to foreclose but utilized by entities that were not part of the transaction. They did not hold the note and deed of trust, or represent any entity or person that did.

Many of the judges understood and would allow my wrongful foreclosure claim to survive a motion for summary judgment brought by the defendants. This motion was intended to convince the court that none of the claims outlined in my complaint could be proven by a preponderance of the evidence. However, if I was right and my claim for wrongful foreclosure was sound, the defendants would ultimately require that the real holder of the note establish that they also were the holder of the deed of trust.

These requirements were provided for in the new bill in the Nevada Senate. It appeared to have been developed after a few other attorneys, and I took on the big banks.

What I ultimately achieved by my complaint was that if there were defects in the foreclosure process, the entity foreclosing would have to rescind its original notice of default and start the foreclosure process all over again under the new statute. [NRS. 598D.100 (1)].

The State Court judges showed some interest in my complaint, but that would not help. Because I did not have any Nevada residents as defendants, the bank's attorneys would move all my cases to federal court. Federal judges did not have much sympathy for my clients, who had signed notes and were not paying as they had agreed. However, my persistent argument that those foreclosing were not proper parties to start or commence the foreclosure process won the day.

In most courts, all my separate claims were dismissed, save for the "wrongful foreclosure" claim. What that meant was that the owners of the outstanding notes had to start their foreclosures all over again, under the new statute. Some of my cases settled and the client got a reduced amount on the note. Some were offered a modification. Many judges accepted my plea to have transparency in the foreclosure process so that if we went to trial, I would win on wrongful foreclosure. The answer was to simply cancel the original notice of foreclosure and start again.

By that time, my clients were in better financial shape for getting modifications of their loan or were willing to accept the inevitable — the loss of their homes. Many thanked me for the extra time they received to get back on their feet and stay in their homes for up to three years before the ax fell.

The banks' attorneys were shrewd. Some of the courts would make them work harder to dismiss my actions, particularly with respect to the wrongful foreclosure. These cunning lawyers would find a way to shift the cases to federal court, where they would typically be dismissed. The state courts seemed to have more passion for the families that they believed had, in fact, been "lured" into terrible loans. However, of the three primary judges presiding in Northern Nevada only one judge agreed with me.

This federal judge would not dismiss the wrongful foreclosures. He was convinced that those parties issuing the notice of default were not parties to the action.

For all the cases on which he ruled, the original notice of foreclosure would have to be rescinded and a new one issued under the new Nevada statute. Thus, the entities foreclosing would have to prove that they were the holders of both the note and the deed of trust. Sometimes they couldn't, and I could settle the case by their reducing the note to the present value of the house.

I saved around 18 homes. That was only about 10 percent of the cases I filed, but the results were deeply satisfying.

These last years of 70-hour workweeks reminded me of long days in the saddle. All the things I learned as a cowboy and a warrior played a part in my dealings with the bank attorneys. They would hit me with a

request for production of documents, admissions, and depositions of my client. Still, I always stayed ahead and did not default on a single case.
During this fight against the banks, I was continuing my own battle with the SEC over my being named in a civil action. I finally had to settle the case against me by confessing to a civil judgment. This would later bring me to the end of my lawyer days.
After three years, while I was dealing with the predatory lending cases and the SEC, the State Bar got involved in my life. Just as I settled the last of my complaints against the banks, the State Bar Association decided to file a complaint regarding a violation of ethical rules because I had confessed to a civil judgment for securities violations. After the battle with the SEC, I decided not to fight the State Bar too, so I simply resigned from it and retire.

Over 35 years as a lawyer, I had completed challenges as an assistant district attorney, as a private practice attorney with public defender contracts, as in-house counsel for the mining company, and finally as a vigilante pursuing predatory lending litigation.

Though my decision to get involved with the mining company turned out to be an injurious one, after so many years of aggressive litigation trial practice, it was time to take down my "shingle," retire my law practice and resign from the State Bar. Now, I can write about it all!

# REFLECTING

As I write the final pages of this memoir, I have reached into my deepest memories to lead you through my journey as a cowboy, a warrior, and a lawyer. Telling these stories has brought to life both the splendor and hardships of ranch life. Disclosing the difficult decision to become an aggressive combat scout pilot reminds me of the sacrifices of those who went to war before me, and who may still have to go. Being a warrior permanently changed my life. My lawyer stories, whether hilarious or sad, reveal the conflicts of a county lawyer handling predicaments faced by civil and criminal defense clients. I related my quest to right the wrongs done by the banks, and described the fight with the government that ultimately ended my career.

Do you feel yourself being hoisted into the saddle? Smelling the sweat of the horse and seeing how the saddle's beautiful tan hue, the one it had when it was new, is now almost black? The horse glances at you as you mount as if to evaluate your skill as a horseman.

Can you hear the ringing of the spurs, the snap of the chaps against the side of the horse as you swing aboard? Do these smells, sights, and sounds linger in your mind?

Do you recall riding out in the early morning, just after sunrise, when it is coldest, and feeling the stillness of the desert? Who could forget the dancing colors of the sky as the sun peeks over the majestic mountains of Toiyabe National Forest? Don't you want to go to Nevada now, where the sagebrush is in bloom? It is not a desert, but a garden. The dust devils dance, but just over the hill, a blinding sandstorm may lurk. And never forget the diamond stars lighting up the night sky, offering a reminder that you are but a mere grain of sand in the scheme of things!

What a vision of the blistering heat and blinding sandstorms. Then, moving cows into the highlands, where fresh mountain streams glitter and the rainbow trout dart away as the horse wades, disturbing the calm waters. The cowboy can sleep away the hot afternoons in a meadow.

All these pleasant and unpleasant thoughts remind us of the stamina and fortitude required of the range cowboys of central Nevada. The small ranches developed by homesteaders still stand here, where families work together from sunrise to sunset.

When you're sipping your beer or iced tea and savoring a barbecued steak, you can now tell your guests about how the men and women of the Nevada desert cattle ranches raised the meat and got it to market. The journey of the cowboy brought this truth home to me and now to you!

Can you smell the gunpowder sticking to your skin, mixing with sweat and tears, filling your nostrils so that you can't breathe? Are your ears still ringing, even though you're wearing a helmet, as the bullets crack from the barrel of the minigun on your left and the gunner's M60 on your right?

Do you hear the frantic call over the radio? "Taking fire…going down…enemy machine gun at my 2 o'clock…dropping smoke!"

We joked to cover our fear as we went out each day, knowing that our job was to find and destroy the enemy.

Then there is the end of the day. You return to your bunk in your hootch and see the empty bed, and hanging alone on the wall is the calvary hat, never to be worn again. Having to write the dreaded letter to the family back home. All these sights, smells, and emotions tell the truth about war.

It's been hard for me to discuss my inner conflicts, developed as days turned to weeks and weeks to months. I meant to shed light on the truth of war known only to those of us who have been there. How truly we are changed. My goal was not only to release my deepest secrets but to explain something about war that you might not have understood.

The goal of my disclosure is the knowledge that when you hear about that returning soldier who struggles to fit back into society, you will find ways to help him or her.

I felt shame in writing the truth about some of the things I did, but it has helped me. I believe you may now see our soldiers in a different way. Unless you were there with them, how else would you know how terrible it was? War changes us forever!

How could anyone now be skeptical about the existence of post-traumatic stress disorder? Men and women go from house to house, not knowing which individual is the good guy or the bad guy. They are always expecting a land mine or booby trap. Then they come home genuinely grieved by what they did and what they saw.

How does that desk clerk at Macy's, or the kid working at the gas station, live with these memories? What can be done to help that completely changed man or woman cope with the memories and go on? The anger and hatred that are developed in war do not instantly go away when the soldier returns home. Never forget to thank someone who has served his or her nation in a war.

I was much luckier than many. The cowboy experience prepared me for the dangers. My years on the ranch, being aware of what could happen, gave me a leg up. My ability to work hard to become a flight instructor, then work during the day and go to night school to get my law degree, kept me from going crazy. I was able to spend half my life working in the justice system. Serving my clients gave me a sense of giving, which helped me make some amends for those terrible things I did during the war. How can we reach out to rehabilitate those broken souls returning from war and show them our gratitude?

I implore you to not just put this book on a shelf and forget about it. Act on what you now know, or on what this book has brought back to your memory.

My memories included sharing the remarkable events in the life of a country lawyer. Can't you see yourself traveling hundreds of miles a day from courtroom to courtroom in the vast desert of central Nevada, then scurrying up the stairs to face the judge and opposing counsel? Feeling the bitterness in the divorce and child custody disputes that sometimes ended in murder?

Some of us love a new challenge. The country bumpkin is facing the seasoned city lawyer, able to not only succeed in saving homes from foreclosure but to also help the legislature change the law to protect the homeowner.

How tense is the art of persuasion when one is prosecuting and defending those most egregious of cases, seeking to deliver justice? Knowing that the element of truth exists, and that often judges or investigators cross the line. Still, it's great to know that an injustice may be corrected by a higher court when a constitutional violation is discovered!

My learning experiences on the ranch helped me learn about the consequences of my actions. The hard lessons I learned as a combat pilot allowed me to survive, but the consequence was a temporary loss of my love for humanity.

Finally, my decision to join a mining company and take on the government had a consequence as well. I would accept my fate and confess to a civil judgment rather than continue battling. This led to the state bar association believing that such conduct was a violation of the ethics rules of professional conduct. I again accepted the consequences and decided not to fight anymore. I would simply resign and retire may practice. My willingness to face the consequences of my actions created the resolve I now possess.

Joining my journey has allowed you to evaluate how I relied on learned skills and the incredible ability to intuitively choose the right action...or maybe it was just plain luck, good or bad.

During this journey, I did not try to hide anything. I fought to disclose everything — right and wrong — that I did as a cowboy, a warrior, and a lawyer. I now end this book as I started it — telling you that we cannot take life too seriously. To quote Aerosmith's "Amazing":

> I kept the right ones out
> And let the wrong ones in
> Had an angel of mercy to see me
> through all my sins
> There were times in my life
> When I was goin' insane
> Tryin' to walk through
> The pain
> Life's a journey, not a destination
> And I just can't tell just what
> tomorrow brings

www.ingramcontent.com/pod-product-compliance
Lightning Source LLC
Chambersburg PA
CBHW041429300426
44114CB00002B/10